AF481336

Modern Day Polymath

How to learn better, study effectively, master skills, build habits & become smarter

Copyright © 2024 Arman N. Chowdhury

All rights reserved. This book or any portion thereof may not be reproduced or used in any manner whatsoever without the express written permission of the publisher except for the use of brief quotations in a book review.

Printed in the United States of America- First Printing, 2022

https://www.armanitalks.com

CONTENTS

Author's Preface 4

Who is the Polymath? 11

Why Personality Matters 16

Finding Meaningful Information 21

How to Know Yourself 25

Why We Are Practicing 34

Evolution 38

General Feel 40

Funnels and Flywheels 44

Internet and Media Literacy 49

Quality Information from Crap 56

Taking Advice: Yay or Nay? 60

Mind of an Autodidact 67

Exercising your Memory 72

Mental Workout 79

Building Systems 80

Designing the Kingpin 86

Brain-Heart Connection 92

Problem Solving 101 99

The Scientific Method 105

Anecdotes 112

How to Create Anecdotes 115

Leveraging Neuroscience to Your Favor 118

How to Execute Deliberate Practice 122

Creating a Feedback System 130

Failing, Gathering Data and Refining 136

Dwelling 142

The Art of Teaching 146

The Art of Explaining Things Clearly 151

Asking Questions & Answering Questions 155

Solidifying Habits 161

End Each Day a Bit Smarter 164

Playing Dumb 168

The Art of Reviewing the Fundamentals 173

Unlearning 178

Global Conversations 185

Incrementally Rewiring your Reality 190

Lifelong Ambition 196

All Emotions are Good Emotions 203

Focus 211

Concentration Challenge 214

Breakdown of the Concentration Challenge 215

Unleashing Genius Potential 219

Pursue Curiosity for Life 222

Closing Thoughts on The Modern-Day Polymath 225

Afterward 228

Author's Preface

Growing up, I wasn't the best kid in terms of tests. I was the hard worker who would do his homework and study hard for the tests.

But on the actual test day? **Subpar scores at best.**

I looked around and saw the smart kids and their behaviors. There were 4 kids in 8th grade who stuck out. They were all the mythical smart kids.
Eric, Junior, Nathan…and Victor.

Victor was different from the other 3. He was a kid from a third world country, I can't recall the exact spot.

Eric, Junior, and Nathan were vocal about how they were the top tier students in class. Each of them would raise their hand when a difficult question was asked to make it visible that they were in a different league.

While Victor was silent and calculative.

Victor had a combover and would wear khaki shorts and a collared shirt.

One time, I sat next to him in class, and we started to talk. I was surprised that he was talking to me because he wouldn't talk to any of the other kids. I was shy, so I guess that's why he felt comfortable around me.

Victor told me that he came from a 3rd world country where his father was murdered for unpaid debts. He was left with his mom and sister. They were able to escape their 3rd world country last minute because the paperwork went through.

He saw robberies, murders & kidnappings throughout his childhood.

I was surprised how brutal this kid's upbringing was. Why was he telling me this? And more importantly…how was he able to still thrive?

Victor and I were in the gifted curriculum which was an accelerated learning program in our school. One common trait of the gifted students was that they were respectful towards the teachers.

But every now and then, the gifted kids would get placed with the regular kids.

The regular classes were the Wild Wild West.
Pure chaos.

These kids would yell a lot, make fun of the teachers, and play pranks on each other.

When it was time for their schoolwork to be turned in, they submitted poor quality work. In return, they were given Cs, Ds & Fs.

Rather than take accountability for their performance, they'd blame others!

They'd blame their teachers.
They'd blame their skin color.
They'd blame their life at home.

They'd blame everyone but themselves.

This was a moment that showed me how different people handled circumstances in different ways.

Victor separated himself from the other 3 smart kids in our class. He also separated himself from the regular kids with the poor work ethic.

Victor never complained.
Pain only strengthened him.

Although Victor was smart, I wouldn't consider him real world smart.
'Why not?'
He was too quiet.

I have nothing against quiet people. But I think to become a real-world genius, you need to be versatile.

That's why I've never been a big fan of tests.
I hate tests.

I think it's smarter to see how someone thrives in group assignments. Do they play their part or are they the dead weight who does nothing & shows up at the end to take credit?

I'm sure Victor would have succeeded in group assignments.
However, I want to stress that real world smarts are beyond tests alone. Unfortunately, there are too many people in the real world that have the school paradigm.

They are like a track horse who has their blinders on, so they don't go off track. The blinders guide the horse perfectly when they are in the race.

But after the race is done, they still have the blinders on like a dummy. Bumping into things, hitting the other horses, and wobbling.

Perspective has been reduced.

In the real world, there are so many people who use their test scores as their badge of honor.
They have some degree and are like:
'Look at me fellas, I'm smart!'

Are you really?
You're smart in school.
But if that's your attitude in the real world, then you're no different than the horse who has the blinders on.

It's time to remove the blinders.

There is a genius within us that we can all unlock. Unlocking that genius is the objective of this book.

Your intelligence is not fixed from birth. If you think that's the case, then you won't like this book. Might as well ask for your refund now.

This book will spread the Level Up Mentality, the mindset for infinite growth.

The modern-day polymath is a master of many fields. Not only the theory, but they have the theory & practice on lock.

They are a walking talking Google of their industry.

Where Victor was a silent assassin who strengthened through pain, the modern-day polymath also knows the art of using emotions to their advantage.

They are emotionally resilient, consistent & have the heart of a warrior.

But where Victor failed to interact with others and collaborate…the modern-day polymath is different.

This is the era of interconnectivity.

The ArmaniTalks brand covers soft skills. More specifically:

concentration (Level Up Mentality), public speaking, storytelling, emotional intelligence, creativity, and social skills.

We will be weaving all these soft skills together to give a holistic experience of what learning is about.

The most important concept that this book will teach is that learning is **fun**.

It is not a boring process where you are memorizing a bunch of lifeless information that you have no passion for. Instead, the information is something that is bringing you one step closer to a larger vision.

That's how we are going to sharpen our understanding of information accumulation, information retention & information application.

Without further ado, let's unlock the genius within.

This is the era of the modern-day polymath.

Who is the Polymath?

A polymath is defined as a person with a vast level of knowledge in multiple domains.

When you think of a polymath, who do you think of?

'I think of Benjamin Franklin or Leonardo DaVinci.'

Those are the 2 names that often come to mind when we bring up polymaths.

Do you think you can be a polymath?

'Of course not! That's only for smart people.'

Ah… a limiting belief has been spotted.

Thus far, we have carried the paradigm of school into the real world. What is the paradigm in school of *smart*?

It comes down to:
- Who can get a certain grade for their assignments, exams and homework.

This measurement may help in school, but it's overly simplistic. Grades mean very little in the real world. Focusing predominantly on grades is a fast way to make sure you accomplish nothing great.

In the real world, what matters more is heart, discipline, and curiosity.

So, let me ask you again, do you think you can become a polymath?
'Um…the answer is still, no.'

I know why you said no.
The reason you said no is because you have created a **separation** from the names of Leonardo DaVinci and Benjamin Franklin.

This separation is created due to a brand. A brand is a symbol which holds meaning.

In your mind, you've heard Benjamin Franklin and Leonardo DaVinci being associated with 'genius' for so long that soon as you hear those names, you **immediately** create a distance from them and you.

That's like when someone says, 'Michael Jordan.' Automatically, without any conscious thought, there is a **gap** which is created. This gap displays how Michael Jordan is the symbol of excellence for basketball & how far he is away from you.

That may be true for a physical sport. For physical sports, the rules are stricter.
However, is that the case for creative fields like intelligence?

A genius is defined as someone with:

- Supreme intellectual or creative powers.

People often forget the 2nd half of that definition. Creative powers, otherwise known as **unique thinking**.

This is why you can be a polymath. Creativity is something that is built into a human. We just need to hone this energy in a unique way.

Also, this is why you don't want to adopt the view of intelligence from school. Aimlessly memorizing and using someone else's curriculum is *not* a symbol of creativity.

Creativity is the art of using your own personality on the fundamentals of a field to create something entirely new & unpredictable.

'Armani, what if I'm still in school. Can I still become a polymath?'
Yes, you can.

Because let me give you a secret...

There are a lot of subjects from school that are relevant for someone outside of school.

History, psychology, biology etc.
I'm revisiting these subjects as an adult!!

'Why?'
Because nowadays, I have a vision and I am working towards a goal. When I'm working towards a goal, these subjects randomly show their face.

Anyone who is starting a business is going to have to learn the fundamentals of psychology. They will even get curious about history and other fields from the school curriculum.

You as a student may be like:
- How can I use this information in a meaningful way?

The subjects that you are learning right now can aid you further in terms of being a polymath.

You have the dots; the goal is to connect them.

This book is all inclusive.

Doesn't matter if you're a student or not, the main aim is to understand that we are going to be in learning mode for the rest of our life, whether we want to or not.

Why Personality Matters

The internet.
What exactly is it?
Can you touch it?
Nah…

It's an information storehouse. A library that you can access at will.

The internet is like a category 5 hurricane. It's a storm that's powerful enough to decimate the concentration levels of your mind.

That's why so many people are lost.

They enter this storm without so much as a life vest. That's why they are floating all over the place.

'Can I tame the internet?'
Yes.

You can tame the internet by becoming a polymath. More specifically, a **personality-based** polymath.

'What's a personality-based polymath?'

A personality-based polymath is someone who leads with their personality first. This requires us to understand what personality is.

We are often given a weak definition of 'personality.' A definition that leaves us with more questions than answers.

But something so important to our life should be digested scientifically:

- A personality is a field of forces.

These field of forces include our memory, desires, intellect, and sense of self.

At any point, we can alter our personality. Yet, for some reason, humans have a very static view of personality.

'Why do you think they have a static view?'
Because a static view helps on a societal level, but not on an individual level.

On a societal level, a personality test can help understand where others are, and group them effectively to make meaningful decisions.

But the more you narrow down to the individuals, the less accurate a personality test becomes.

That's when what seemed static becomes dynamic.

It's like the Newtonian world and the Quantum world.

On a Newtonian level, the world around seems predictable and easy to measure. But the more you zone into the tiny world of Quantum, everything becomes a field of forces.

It's the same with personality.

Thus far, we only have a Newtonian view of personality. If we can unlock a Quantum view, that's when the game starts to change.

'How do I unlock a Quantum view of my personality?'

You unlock it by looking at the person across the mirror.

Picture yourself as having 2 bodies.
- *The mental body and the physical body.*

The human is very similar to a word.

For example:

- Apple.

What do you see?
'An apple.'
Be more specific.
'I see the scribbles which create A-p-p-l-e.'

What else do you see?
'An image of an apple in my mind.'

- The scribbles of A-p-p-l-e is a symbol for your physical body.
- The image created by the scribbles is a symbol for your mental body.

The more you understand the mental and physical components of you, the more you understand your personality.

'Um, Armani?
Whatsup.
'What the hell does this have to do with becoming a polymath?'
A ton.

Because the more that you understand yourself, the more the internet turns from a category 5 hurricane into a light drizzle.

'What do you mean?'

It means that you can now spot the meaningful information from the junk.

Finding Meaningful Information

If you try to define 'information', you will become a philosopher overnight. It's a difficult word to describe.

I think it is safe to say in this era, that information naturally doesn't have any value. It has value based on the value that the user assigns to it.

Imagine someone comes to you and says that they have the greatest book ever. However, no one has read it.

If no one has read it, that means that it can't be regarded as the greatest book ever. Even if most people on the planet have read it, besides 1 person, it **still** cannot be regarded as the greatest book ever.

That's because information is participatory. It requires another human.

Therefore, knowing yourself is one of the **keys** to becoming a genius. It allows you to spot relevant information from irrelevant information.

There was time in college when I was struggling. There was a possibility that I was going to get kicked out of the engineering program.

One day, my college advisor pulled me to the side and said:
'Armani, the river did not cut through the rock through force, but through persistence.'

When he told me that quote, my world view had **shifted**. I realized I was trying to bulldoze myself into getting a higher grade. But the minute he told me about the value of persistence, I understood the importance of small daily wins.

That quote saved me from failing out of the engineering program.

A few years later, I had a buddy who was going through a similar issue. I was supposed to help him study.

That's when I said to him:
'John, the river did not cut through the rock through force, but through persistence.'

He took some time to think about the quote. Then he said:

'Armani, that is the stupidest thing I've ever heard in my life. Quit wasting time & help me study bro!'

That showed me the quote did not have any intrinsic value. Instead, it had value that we assigned to it.

To spot relevant information from irrelevant information, we need to find a way to **personalize** the information. This is a skill.

If you do not know yourself, then you will not be able to tame the internet. Everything is going to seem important.

THE INTERNET WILL EAT YOU ALIVE.

Don't you see all these people getting brainwashed like idiots nowadays?

All information is relevant information to them because they know nothing about themselves.

Some exam told them they were an extrovert or an introvert 5 years ago and they accepted it.
They gave one of their most important components (personality) to another group of humans to decide.

Now it's easier to brainwash them by telling them which information is important and which isn't.

The modern-day polymath isn't fooled that easily though. It's because they took the time to understand themselves. Through the process of understanding themselves, it becomes much easier to scope through fluff.

How to Know Yourself

I want to make this universal. The following formula will work whether you're:

- Trying to become smart for school.
- Trying to become valuable for your company.
- An entrepreneur who has no choice but to get smarter. Otherwise, your business will fade away.

Set an infinite goal.

'A what?'

Set an infinite goal.

'What do you mean? I thought I was supposed to set deadlines and all that.'

You can do that with infinite goals.

An infinite goal can adopt the features of finite goals, but the opposite is not always true.

Become like a person who sells books. Let's say that you are an author of a book called 'Purpose 101.'

You write the entire book on Microsoft Word for free. Then you pay a guy on Fiver 450 dollars to format the book & make a cover. Then you upload the book on Amazon to sell.

What next?

You just happen to host a popular YouTube page that talks about purposing purpose. You start promoting the book on your channel and begin getting some sales.

Within a few weeks, you make your 450 dollars back. That means you have recouped your initial expenses.

Want to know something?
'What?'
Every penny that you make after that is infinite ROI.

Infinite ROI is when you have recouped your money on the initial investment and still have your asset cash flowing!

'So?'
Now your mind is capable of grasping what an infinite concept is from a practical vehicle like business.

Me just telling you to envision 'infinity' will make your mind zig zag. But by understanding the infinite ROI example from selling books, the mind can grasp the analogy.

Here's the cool part...
Even though you have understood selling books from an infinite ROI lens, that does not eliminate its finite attributes.

You still have the finite features which show how much money you are making.

In 5 weeks, you made 200 sales.
2,998$ in revenue.
1,358$ in net.
Etc.

The point is that we can view infinite goals in the context of finite measurements as well.

The reason depression hits people is because they have/had finite goals. Unfortunately, they were taught goal setting by marketing narratives & mainstream society.

A lot of troubles happen because people are sold marketing messages that they perceive as a legitimate lifestyle.

One of the popular marketing messages is when you're retired at age 65 and drinking sour amaretto's at a beach. You've 'made it.'

However, that's not how a human works. It's because humans are meant to work.

Working is a feature of humans just as much as their eyelids, toenails, and fingers.

Having a finite goal towards work is similar to asking a silly question like:
'When can I stop trimming my toenails?'
Fool! You cut your toenails for the rest of your life.

We **need** to create an infinite goal.

'How do I set an infinite goal?'
We set an infinite goal by:
1. Making it exceedingly grand.
2. Using a general word.
3. Both.

Let's say you are a doctor who sets the goal of:

- I'll become the greatest doctor of all time, forever.

Not only is that a grand goal… But adding 'forever' to anything makes it an infinite goal.

The infinite goal is what will eventually allow different information to make sense.

This doctor will be able to PERCEIVE data in an otherworldly sort of way.

This method was used by a lot of top tier athletes. They'd say:
'I want to become the best boxer of all time.'

This goal may not be purely infinite, but it sure as a hell is grand. With it being grand, they will **perceive** information in a completely different way.

THE GRANDER THE GOAL, THE MORE OUR PARADIGM OPENS.

The blinders come off…

Remember what we said earlier:

- Information by itself means nothing. It means something when we assign value to it.

When we have a grand goal, all knowledge connects.

To give you an example:

- Roy Jones Junior is one of the greatest boxers of all time.

You better believe that his goal was to become the greatest from the very beginning.

A logical mind who only sets finite goals will be like: 'I'm sure Roy only learned from other boxers.'

Nope!

Roy learned from animals as well.

He'd intently watch how lions hunted gazelles. By watching that, he was able to refine his striking for boxing.

As for my life, I deal with ArmaniTalks, which is a storytelling business. I create content on improving communication skills through YouTube videos, books, blogs, classes and much more.

I noticed that traditional business advice doesn't resonate with me. It seems like too many people are focused on quick payouts and the tactics rather than building a brand and working on the fundamentals.

'So, what did you do?'
I studied farmers.
'You did what???'
I studied farmers.

I'm not sure if you know this, but there are a lot of resources online for farmers. Well, I watched some interviews of farmers to see how they went about their grind.

That's when they talked about the importance of having a long-term mindset.

- Plant the seed.
- Continue to water it.
- And one day, the seed will blossom into a plant.

That's when I noticed a stunning insight!

- I create content which is equivalent to planting a digital seed.
- I water it by marketing it.

- And one day, the content will blossom into cashflow.

Identical concepts.

I noticed the more advanced information technology became, the more we were going back to the agrarian age. I guarantee if you have a business of some sort, learning the basics of farming will help you master your craft!

I wouldn't have been able to see the subtle parallel of seeds and content if I was only setting finite goals. My perception would not have opened.

Our perception is stubborn. It needs to be bulldozed open!

Therefore, set an infinite goal.

Here are a few more examples:

- I'm a flawless student.
- I'll become the greatest realtor in the universe.
- I'm an impeccable writer.

It needs to appeal to **your** identity.

If you say something like:

- I'll become a flawless nurse.

But you don't know diddly squat about nursing, then there will be dead feelings.

'Are feelings that important for learning? I thought I was only supposed to use logic?'
No, big mistake!!

Curiosity often comes in feelings.

We'll talk about how to leverage feelings to build bulletproof concentration levels and thick skin later.

For the time being, phrase the correct infinite goal. You know it's right for you when you have a surge of feelings. Keep playing around with the phrasing till you find that sweet spot.

Become infinite in the mind and you will soon become infinite in your movements.

Why We Are Practicing

When I first started the ArmaniTalks podcast, I thought there were only a few different voices out there:

- Loud, soft, and middle of loud and soft.

That's when I began recording more episodes.
'Learned anything?'
Yes.
'What?'
There were *infinite* vocal options.

A podcast is recorded on an audio software like Audacity. You will see your voice when you speak into the microphone and see an audio recording on the screen.

NO 2 AUDIO WAVES ARE THE SAME.

The more you practice, the more you can perceive the micro differences. This is why we are practicing the information that we learn.

- The goal is to become infinite in our movements.

With this goal, when we practice over time, we begin to surprise ourselves.

Do you think a chess player understands every possible move to make? No.

They know that the more games they get under their belt, the more confused they will be (in a good way).

There is good confusion and bad confusion just like there are good failures and bad failures.

A good failure is when you are trying something new, failing, and gathering more data.
A bad failure is when you keep making the same silly mistakes repeatedly without correcting.

A good confusion is when you are confused about what to do next. This causes your mind to be challenged & unleash peak curiosity.
A bad confusion is when you have been confused about the same topic for very long without trying to learn more about it. Rather than learning more about it, you've developed a bitter & hopeless attitude regarding the subject.

The more we practice, the more we are going to keep discovering new things that we can implement. That's why we set the intention from the get-go of having an infinite perspective regarding goals.

- If you set a finite goal, then practicing will feel like a chore.
- If you set an infinite goal, then practicing feels like a fun scavenger hunt.

I always found it weird when someone said:
'I have no motivation to learn.'

After hearing that sentence from different people around the world, that's when I learned it was a common issue. The issue occurs because people had no clue how to learn. They had this illusion that they would:

- Figure things out.

When you think you will eventually *figure it out*, it's one of the most dangerous traits for someone with a self-taught mindset.

The modern-day polymath remains a lifelong beginner.

Thinking you have 'figured it out' is a state of thinking that happens in the formal atmosphere.

- The state of being given an A.
- The state of being given a diploma.
- The state of being given a pat on the back for finishing a group project.

But in the real world, *finish* is an illusion.

Does a successful business owner say:
'Okay, looks like I figured it out. No more innovation needed for my business!'

Nope.

It's because humans need to evolve. Evolution and the modern-day polymath go hand in hand.

Evolution

The 2 ways for humans to evolve:
1. Collect nodes (information).
   - Collecting nodes happens through introspection, experiencing, studying and learning.
2. Connect nodes (creativity).
   - Connecting nodes happens through writing, speaking, teaching, and introspecting.

The is when we see parallels between humans and information systems. A system is an interconnection of parts that lead to something new.

With complex systems, there are only 2 options:

- Evolve

or

- Devolve

Maintaining is an illusion.

'Why does it seem like I'm capable of maintaining?' It feels like that because you have a limited point of view.

- Some days, you are evolving.
- Some days, you are devolving.

This creates the illusion of maintenance.

With the perspective of information systems, evolving into a modern-day polymath seems like a no brainer.

The days of being good at only thing is a thing of the past. Nowadays, it's all about becoming a master of many fields.

The purpose of life is to evolve.

My friend, set an infinite goal and evolve towards it daily.

General Feel

When it comes down to absorbing information, start off general.

Imagine there is a guy named Gustavo who knows nothing about Eastern philosophy.

How would he learn a topic like this?

First thing he should assess is his curiosity. Learning a field that you are already curious about helps way more than forcing yourself to be curious about it.

Can you force yourself to be curious? Sure. But it's the best situation when the curiosity is already there. But Gustavo's curiosity is not already there.

Should Gustavo immediately get a textbook and start deep diving into the field?

Yes, if he wants to make learning feel like a pain in the butt...

Our strategy is to get a feel for the topic first.

'What do you mean get a feel for the topic?'
Understand it on a general scope. Get the bird's eye view, then go detailed.

If I were Gustavo, I would get acquainted from multiple different sources that discuss Eastern philosophy.

This is when we are not discriminating at all. Gustavo doesn't care who is legit and who is not legit, yet. Gustavo's main purpose is to **understand the language of the field.**

That's how a lot of learning happens:
Through language.

Gustavo is consuming random blogs on the topic, YouTube videos, podcasts and much more.

After getting a general feel, he understands the field from a **high level**.

Let's say he learns about consciousness, spiritual disciplines, karma and much more.

Once he has a general understanding, that's when he begins narrowing down.

You ever seen a funnel before?

A funnel starts off wide and gets narrow. If I wanted to put a sand from a bucket into a water bottle, then I need to place the funnel in the bottle. Then I'd gently pour the sand from the bucket into the entrance of the funnel, so it pours into the bottle.

Much more effective than just pouring the bucket of sand straight into the bottle.

- The bucket of sand represents the subject.
- The bottle represents our mind.
- The funnel represents the strategy of going from general to specific.

Let's do one more analogy.

Gustavo not only needs to learn Eastern philosophy, but he also wants to start settling down for marriage.

You're his dating coach.

Gustavo notifies you that he hasn't had a date in 15 years.

Are you going to tell him to get married to the first girl he goes on a date with?

Unless he really resonates with the girl, then the answer is…hell no!

You will tell him to go on a few dates to get a general feel for what he likes and doesn't like. Once he gets a general understanding of what he wants, then it's easier to narrow down.

This is similar to how we familiarize ourselves with topics.

Start wide & keep getting narrower.

Funnels and Flywheels

- Funnels start off wide and narrow down.
- Flywheels are when we get the output and feed it back as an input to gain momentum.

By combining the funnels and flywheels forever, we are capable of learning forever.

The average person goes through 1 funnel and says: 'Looks like I have this subject figured out.'

Using language liked 'figured out' means that this person has set a finite goal rather than an infinite goal. There learning will end.

The modern-day polymath plays infinite games for life.

With this infinite game, they realize the end of one funnel is the beginning of another funnel.

As an adult, how would you study the subjects you learned in school?

Let's start with the basics: History, psychology & social studies.

You start off with history. That's when you start getting a general **feel** for the subject.

Maybe getting a few textbooks, listening to a couple of podcasts, watching YouTube videos to see who the bigger players were. You start developing a general theme of the subject.

You eventually look into politics. That's when you learn about the President, how congress works, dictatorships and more.

As you are winding down to the end of the funnel, that's when you think you can clearly explain the subject to someone else.

I have the podcast test.
'Which is?'
Can you create 1 funny podcast episode on the subject?

The reason we want it to be funny is because this forces you to explain the subject in simple language. Simple language shows clarity in the field.

Try it out for yourself.

We can only compress the subject if we really know the topic.

Did you pass the podcast test?
Excellent! You've made it to the end of the history funnel.

'Wow! Yes, I can't believe I know history.'
Not quite.

Were you confused on anything?
Confusion is one of the **best** things for a polymath. That means we are about to get the output and new input.

'Yes, I was confused regarding the mindsets of a few presidents and why they did what they did.'
Can you be a little bit more specific?
'Not really. I was just confused regarding mindset.'
That's fine.

This is when we activate our flywheel. Get the output of your knowledge from history and input it into the new flywheel.

What comes to mind when you think of mindset?
'Psychology.'

Correct!

So, you started off at the history funnel, went wide, then narrowed down. Once you reached the output, you inputted the understanding of history into the brand-new funnel of psychology.

The funnel and flywheel have been activated.

Now you execute the same strategy with the new funnel.
- Start wide and narrow down.

Learn some of the basic language such as the ego, super ego, subconscious mind etc.

The more you learn about the field, the more you will find yourself hopping into another funnel.

Learning is messy & elegant at the same time.

In the real world, you aren't only going through 1 funnel at a time. You'll often find yourself activating multiple funnels at once. This is known as interleaving learning. When you learn about multiple fields simultaneously.

The modern-day polymath views learning as the merging of faith with the intellect.

'Faith and intellect? Aren't the 2 completely different?'

Not quite.

You entering another funnel is an act of faith. You should know that you are going on a journey.

Often, you'll start off at history and find yourself somewhere in the biology funnel.

This is when you have faith to acknowledge that you are collecting a bunch of dots to only connect them later. Then as you collect more and more dots, you will intellectually and logically be able to connect them.

The process of activating a funnel and outputting the understanding into the next funnel is where the world of faith and logic merge.

This is the way of funnels and flywheels.

Internet and Media Literacy

Don't be fooled…

Just because we are going from funnel to funnel does not mean we are consuming all quality content.

Often, a polymath is entering uncharted territory.

The less you know anyone that is studying in a field, the more difficult it is to ask for recommendations.

When it's super uncharted, that's when you start off consuming all people's content. Reliable people from the beginning later get discovered as scammers, deceits, and frauds.

Which is why we are going wide.

The wider we are in the beginning stage, the less likely we are to get mesmerized by one source alone.

View surfing the internet as a skill.

'A skill?? I surf the internet all the time. I never knew I had a skill!'

It's because you probably don't.

A ton of people who are surfing the internet are not doing it with any sort of intent. They just get spoon fed random information and take it as 'facts.'

The modern-day polymath treats the internet as a friend.
An interactive friend.

Ask the internet the right questions and it will give you the right responses.

When you just type in *dog*, what do you get?
'I get articles of dogs.'
Very general, right?
'Right.'

Let's say you have a dog, and your dog has been throwing up recently. So, you type in Google:
'Dog has been throwing up.'
That's when you're going to get much more targeted articles. Articles which discuss dogs throwing up.

Although the phase *dogs* is there, we are seeing different information.

However, from your context, that's still not enough.

You realize your dog isn't always throwing up. Instead, it's only throwing up when it eats a particular dog food.

Now you can get even more specific with your query.
'Why does my dog throw up when it eats food X?'

This is when you will get even more specific articles. Most don't make it that far. It's because they are too passive with the internet. They don't participate with it like an interactive friend.

A polymath views the internet as a friend and a loyal tool. Therefore, they understand the pros and cons.

To build the ability to ask the right questions and query the correct key phrases, you need to practice. It takes going through a lot of wrong content to get to the right content.

Earlier, we were giving an example of Gustavo learning Eastern philosophy. Let's say he stumbles across a few articles.

The articles on the first page are getting the most love from Google. If Google recommends an article on the first page, that means they view it as an authority page.

As Gustavo is reading the articles on Eastern philosophy, he's happy…but not that happy. He feels like something is missing.

Most of the articles are of Westerners trying to sell him something. They give some relevant information, but nothing that meaningful.

So, Gustavo does something he rarely does.
'What's that?'
He clicks the 2nd page, the 3rd page and 4th page.

That's when he starts seeing articles of Swami's with in-depth content talking about Eastern philosophy. These articles are placed in the later pages of the search engine.

However, is it valuable?
YES!!

That's a lesson into the internet. You need to pry and look around. Just because an article is on page 1 does not mean that it is more valuable.

53

Maybe the people on page 1 have okay content but an amazing SEO team while the later pages have great content but no SEO team. It's a miracle they are even on page 4!

Get the right content that will propel you towards your infinite goal. This is where media literacy comes in.

Media literacy is the ability to create, curate and consume content with intent.

Someone with average media literacy does not see nuances.

Let's view it as a spectrum.

A person with idiotic media literary says:
'If it's on the internet, then it must be true!'

They have very little understanding.

Someone in the middle category creates content. This allows them to spot the duds from the studs when they are in consumption mode.

However, this group does not have their emotions in check. If they see something that resonates with their philosophy, then they are much more willing to accept it. But if it's content that remotely challenges their worldview, they rule it off.

Someone with high media literacy can create content, spot propaganda & they can change their mind when new information is presented.

It's one thing to say:
'I'll change my mind when new information is presented.'
It's another thing to actually do it!

Don't be so quick to change your mind though. Seek more information.

Media literacy is going to become an important topic because content is subjective. It's easier than ever to find 'evidence' for anything.

Think of the most ridiculous claim out there and type it in Google. You'll see herds of people making a case for the ridiculous claim with their 'facts.'

JUST BECAUSE IT IS ON THE INTERNET DOES NOT MEAN IT IS TRUE.

A dummy will be like:
'Well, why even use the internet then?'
Because it's a **tool**.

There are plenty of times when we have a pen on our desk that looks nice. But when we try using it, it doesn't work properly. The ink is dry.

Does that mean all the pens on the desk are broken? No. This one is broken, and it will require us to test the other pens to find a working one.

Media literacy is built overtime.

Understand that inputs dictate output. If you ask a quality chef what they spend a long time doing…They'll tell you they spend a long-time collecting quality ingredients.

Likewise, we will spend time collecting quality information.

Quality Information from Crap

This section is going to be highly subjective. At max, I can give a few tools, but ultimately, it's all about sharpening your judgment.

'How is judgment sharpened?'
Judgment is sharpened through trial and error. Go through the junk to spot the gold.

One way to spot crap content is when it's an opinion piece that is masquerading as facts.

'Do I stop consuming them?'
This is where I will give a polarizing response. I think all content is good content for the polymath.

'What?? You just said there is crap content. Now you are saying all content is good content?'
Correct.

'Why not completely cut out the crap?'
Let's say you run a team of 10 people.

5 of them love you.

5 of them hate you.

The ones who hate you play an important role in your team. Firing them is not an option because that will cause you to miss a bunch of deadlines.

What do you do then?
Do you completely cut ties with those who hate you?

Let's raise the stakes even more and say the people who hate you plan to overthrow you.

At this point, I'd want to know more about them. What exactly are they plotting?

Me wanting to know more about how they plan to harm me does not negate the fact that they hate me. Being aware of my weak spots helps me out tremendously.

With content, it's a similar philosophy.

Yes, I do not view them as a respectable source. However, I am still capable of seeing what they are sharing so I know what NOT to look for.

This builds emotional intelligence & further sharpens judgment.

Sometimes, due to surface level understanding, we may be quick to be like:
'This is garbage content.'

While later, when we have more information, we are like:
'Wait a minute, the content was not garbage. I just lacked understanding at that stage of my life.'

Other times, you'll see a person you respect swearing that something is junk:
'Don't even bother reading and listening to it. All it will do is waste your time!'

Then you check it out and are like:
'Wait a minute, that was pretty useful!'

That's happened to me a few times. I had a respected friend who said:
'Trust me bro, don't watch Ted Talks. It's a complete waste of time.'

I didn't want to tell him, but I watched Ted Talks. Not every talk was great, but a lot of them left a profound change in me.

One of them was Poet Ali's talk on the language of being a human.

That was a talk that got me to rethink what language really was.

59

Remain open minded & skeptical. You never know when something you considered a dud can help you out later in the game.

Taking Advice: Yay or Nay?

A polymath is knowledgeable in multiple fields. For them to build so much knowledge, they needed to experiment.

There are different platitudes out there that are destructive. One of the platitudes is the one that only talks up mentors.

There are times when getting a mentor too quickly is a destructive thing to do.

That's because a mentor is trying to **save** you time. While a modern-day polymath is trying to **spend** time.

There are 2 types of failures out there:
- The one where you keep making the same mistake (bad).
- The one where you are gathering more data (good).

One of the services I offer in the ArmaniTalks consulting program is learning how to speak on camera.

After 300 plus recorded videos, presentations, digital interviews… speaking to the camera was a skill that I spent *years* cultivating.

One day, I had a client who hated speaking to the camera. He practiced a few videos and said:
'Not sure why, but the videos look very weird.'

I looked at the some of the clips and immediately saw the issue.

'What was it?'
He didn't blink at all.
'How long were the videos?'
5 minutes.
'Yeah right! It's impossible to not blink for 5 minutes without noticing!'

As a matter of fact, when speaking to a camera, it's easy to forget to blink.

I would know because there are a few videos where I didn't blink at all. There would be a few comments saying:

'Yo, this guy doesn't blink at all!'

When I read the comments, I thought:
'What an idiot. Of course, I blinked. Otherwise, my eyes would be tearing up.'

I rewatched the videos to spot the exact moment when I blinked.

And I kept watching.
And watching…
And watching away…

I went through the entire 5 minute plus video to realize I hadn't blinked at all! That's when I learned that you don't have to blink.

Since I went through that experience, I was able to notice my client's quirk immediately.

That's probably an issue that's difficult to Google. Sure, you may find articles on it. But noticing the problem requires reps!

That showed me that spending time & messing up will make you hyper astute with your craft.

'Would you say your client was wrong to hire you? Because shouldn't your client be failing his way to success?'

No, he was not wrong because I saved him time and he was able to adjust. Likewise, I was not aware of speaking without blinking until I received that comment. That comment saved me time.

The insight meant a lot because I had accumulated experience beforehand. Likewise, my client hired me after he built experience beforehand rather than coming as a pure newbie.

A polymath needs to break traditional notions of thinking. Where they think of things as right or wrong.

In the real world, it's more about synergy or dysergy:

- Synergy is when 1 + 1 is more than 2.
- Dysergy is when 1 + 1 is less than 2.

Quality insights are when synergies are forming within.

A poor attitude can prevent a student from learning more:

'I don't have a mentor so I can't begin.'

False.

Since you don't have a mentor, you must begin.

Just know that all advice is not good advice. Advice is something that others need a tamed ego to give. Most people aren't giving advice. What they are doing is recruiting.

Most people are not asking:
1. Where are you?
2. Where do you want to go?
That's advice.

Instead, what they're subliminally saying is:
'You should do this because that's what I did.'

This is going to be a heartbreaking moment for a lot of polymaths. It's because they see that people who they respect fall into the habit of recruiting.

Humans love to give advice as much as they love to ramble.

When a human rambles, it makes them feel the same pleasure as when they have sex. When a human gives advice, they **feel** important.

Bud, all advice seems like good advice when you lack experience. What works for one person may not always work for another person.

Back to the example with my client who was learning to speak on camera.

- When I told him to blink, he blinked.

That advice worked.

But if I said:

'Johnny, you should tell jokes too! People who tell jokes are more engaging.'

That advice may or may not work with the levels of variables that are involved.

- Maybe his field is more serious.
- Maybe he feels terror before joking. So, it's better to work him up with something he is comfortable with.
- Maybe his jokes suck.

Advice becomes more subjective with each variable that is added.

Telling someone to blink is a simple system. Like turning ON or OFF a light switch.

Telling someone to incorporate humor is like debugging a computer.

Much more complex.

Be open minded to hear others out.

Be skeptical of taking everything they say as law.

Mind of an Autodidact

The autodidact is self-taught. The fruits of being self-taught is to become a polymath.

To understand how the mind of an autodidact works, we need to notice the subtle differences from a street smarts primed mind vs a book smarts primed mind.

Most of education comes down to 3 different components:
- Theory
- Reasoning
- Experience

How they are prioritized will determine what type of mindset you have.

In formal education, the order of importance is:
1. Theory
2. Reasoning
3. Experience

You are first given the theory. Otherwise, known as the formulas, rules, and concepts for that field.

Then you are expected to reason through the theory (tests and homework). Reasoning is when you make logical conclusions with the information at hand.

Finally, the icing on the cake is the experience. The phrase *icing on the cake* implies that it's great if you have it, but it's not really needed.

In formal education, the theory is the cake.

For the mindset of an autodidact, it's flipped. The order of importance is:
1. Experience
2. Reasoning
3. Theory

The autodidact may get some theory to get started. But for them, experience is the cake.

Are they getting firsthand experience in this field?

Then, when they reason, they use their experience and make logical conclusions from that.

Finally, they fill in the gaps of understanding with additional theory.

Which sort of mindset are you?

The 2 mindsets are not completely independent from one another.

During undergrad, I got an electrical engineering degree. This was formal education.

First, I was given a bunch of theory, and expected to learn the formulas for voltage, capacitors, batteries etc.

Then, I was tested on this material to measure my reasoning skills.

Finally, in the closing 2 years of school, I was given firsthand experience with labs.

On the other hand, my journey with public speaking followed a different path.

I started off getting firsthand public speaking experience by joining Toastmasters (a public speaking club).

After some time, I was able to reason from the database of my experiences.

- Breathing fast? That means speech anxiety is on the rise.
- Feeling unconfident on stage? Be sure to dress up.
- You only need to look at 3 of the audience members as a beginner. One from left, middle and right.

Finally, as a few years went by, I began working with a public speaking coach. In our first meeting, he gave me his book to read as an assignment.

As I read his book, I learned the theory of public speaking. A lot of what I thought was unique to me were also principles experienced by other speakers.

In the field of electrical engineering, the path was formal. In the field of public speaking, the path was informal.

As an autodidact, you don't have to pin 1 side against the other side. It's best if you can make both sides complement one another!

As I began public speaking, I noticed a stunning parallel between human beings and electrical communication systems.

An electrical communication system has a sender and a receiver. The sender gets the message, encodes it by converting it to signals and transfers it through a medium. The receiver receives message, decodes the message, and processes it. The objective is to keep the noise down (junk information) and keep the signal high (meaningful information).

That's very similar to how public speaking works.

There is a speaker (sender) and an audience (receiver). The speaker gathers the thoughts from their mind and encodes it into words. The words are sent through the medium of air. The audience receives the words and decodes the message to process it.

By using my teaching from formal education, I was able to make my public speaking journey much easier.

Can you do that was well?
Can you cross combine formal & informal education?

There is no such thing as complete blank slate in the world of knowledge. All experiences intertwine and get a remix down the line.

Exercising your Memory

'What are your thoughts on taking notes?'
I think taking notes may help for certain fields. But I would urge a person to not underestimate the power of their memory.

The memory is infinite.
There's no end to the amount of information that can be stored. Creative geniuses have a reservoir of data and information in their memory.

'How does someone go about building their memory?'
By constantly working it out.

It's one thing to have concepts in your database. But unless you **recall** the information and **personalize** it, that information will eventually fade away.

The beauty regarding recalling memory is that it leads to chemical changes in the brain...
You'll feel it.

This is much different than someone who just reads off notes.

Most people take notes like cowards.

Whether they outright say it or not, they undermine the power of their memory when taking notes. Which is why the notes are overly detailed.

It's much better to have a general understanding of the topic first. Get a general feel by activating the funnels & flywheels beforehand.

Then when you are in a situation where taking notes is optional, you can jot down the most important information. When you have a general feel for the topic, that's when the intelligence in the body is awakened.

'Intelligence in the body??'
Yes. The mind thinks, the body knows.

You'll see the body is alerting you in certain moments:
'Yo, is this information important? Nah. But that information is important.'

By:
1. Having a general understanding of the topic.

2. Having your body alert you of the important points.

You take *effective* notes.

The memory is only built from the information that is recalled. Not only recalled once but recalled repeatedly.

This is when learning and memory become blended with the personality.

Without a purpose, all information will seem important. But with a purpose, you can seamlessly scope through the fluff.

Here are the 4 components of the mind:
- Intellect
- Ego
- Memory
- Sensory processing system

The *intellect* uses logic. Rapid rates of true and false decisions.

Ego is your identity. This is the narratives that you are sold on.

Memory is the data of your experiences and the knowledge you consumed.

And *sensory processing system* allows you to see separate objects. An example is the computer screen. Although all the folders on the computer screen is just light, it looks like different clickable files. That's how the mind works. It turns the lights of electromagnetic waves into separateness.

Identity (ego) is something that is **very** important.

If you personalize information to the identity, then it's impossible to forget information. However, appealing too much to the identity may make you biased.

A lot of politicians know this. They know that the people who they are trying to get votes from have some narrative that they are sold on.

Let's say a community is all about defunding the police.

The politician will start off with the narrative of defunding the police and activate the **identity** proportion of their brains.

Once the politician places themselves as anti-police to the 'defund police' crowd, the crowd will view the politician in a positive light.

Control the emotions and it's much easier to control their intellect. When the identity and the intellect are in conflict, the identity often wins.

If this same politician goes up to a group of people who loves law enforcement, then he will not be able to get away with the same narrative of defunding the police.

Identity plays a big role in information processing.

This is important to know because you can leverage the identity to unleash supreme memory.

If you're learning about personal finance because you think that's what you're supposed to do, that doesn't really appeal to **your identity** that much.

But if you are learning personal finance because your business is your life, now your identity gets engaged.

This business that you started was the only thing that kept you going when your back was against the wall. You bet on yourself and took a risk to make sure that the business succeeds.

As the business scaled, you noticed there were accounting errors. Now you want to learn the personal finance side of things to keep your baby alive and strong.

How compelling!
What a better narrative than *'oh, I'm learning personal finance because I'm supposed to.'*

When you get your identity involved, the memory becomes your servant.

It's best to learn something you want to learn vs something you have to learn.

This should be common sense. Still, it needed to be said.

There is an ancient philosophy which states that the fire does not light wet wood. But when a match meets dry wood, fire runs ablaze.
- The wet wood represents a mind that is not curious.

- The dry wood represents a mind that is curious.

The curious mind leads to absorbing information at rapid rates because curiosity implies that the identity is engaged.

Would you want to hear gossip about people you have never heard of, or people you know? Or better yet, let's say someone says:

'You won't believe what Jesse was saying about you. Never mind, I can't tell you.'

This will get your mind hyper curious because it appeals to your identity.

Every now and then, we may have to learn something that we don't see appealing to our identity.

Find a way to turn this boring topic into a relevant topic for your identity. View it as a puzzle.

- If you can turn boring tasks into fun tasks, then you will become unstoppable.
- If you can turn any subject into a subject that appeals to your identity, then you will become a genius.

Mental Workout

Find 3 topics that you know very little about and see how they can tie into your life.

Don't pick something super obvious like technology or money.

Go general.

If you can't find anything, then think about:

- The lunar eclipse
- Motorcycle helmets
- Coral reefs

You can't make something connect to your identity if you know nothing about it. So, spend time getting a general feel for the topic and see how it appeals to your identity.

The process of seeing how it's relevant to you will **flex** your creativity.

Building Systems

Experience is key.

Without experience, we become just another guy who has high test scores.

Question is, what are we actively building?

It can be a variety of things, but we need to build a complex system. This is a system that we are going to work on forever.

'Forever?? Then when will I ever take a break?'

Never.

This may seem like a daunting task, but it isn't. Subjects are built to be worked on forever.

I know a professional body builder who is like:

'I've been at this for 15 years and still am learning something new every day.'

Think about the variables that are involved:

- Nutrition
- Sleep
- Workout regiment
- Supplements

And this is still scratching the surface.

The body is a temple that we own for the rest of our lives. If you have no clue what to build, then start off with the body.

'Are you really saying that I can become a modern-day polymath by working out more?'
With the correct strategy, yes.

It's because you are building real world experience and becoming curious about a variety of fields.

Tons of lifters talk like scientists, not the traditional 'meat heads' that's shown on media.

Why?
It's because they are becoming a master of their craft. To become a master of the craft comes down to building something.

In the process of building is where systems thinking is unlocked.

Systems allow you to see the bigger picture. This is much different than the traditional types of thinking that we are used to. In the standard school system, the main form of thinking is known as node thinking.

Systems thinking is when you collect nodes and interconnect nodes.

- Nodes are the parts.
- Interconnecting nodes is connecting the parts in a useful way.

A person who is building their body is collecting the right food, knowledge, supplements and much more. They are going to have to troubleshoot their way into success. There is no such thing as completely figuring it out.

For example:
There are moments when a professional body builder is getting their muscles growing. Suddenly, they notice themselves feeling stiff. What now?

Now they do targeted research on what to do when they're feeling stiff & unable to have a wide range of motion.

In the process of researching, they are collecting more nodes to create more interconnections of understanding. The lifter studies topics on yoga, drinking more water, switching up the workouts etc.

After incorporating some yoga, they feel better. Along with feeling better, they now understand how stretching will help them build their flexibility and further enhance their body.

The student suddenly sees a connection between mass gain and stretching. Would this person have been able to point the connection beforehand?

Possibly.

But the connection became **real** when he felt the muscle spasms of being inflexible & soothing those spams with the incorporation of yoga.

Another example is gardening.

'Gardening? First you say body building and now you are saying I can do gardening to become a modern-day polymath?'
It doesn't matter what you build as long as it is complex.

Build a complex system not a simple system.

'What's the difference?'

The difference lies in the degrees of parts and interconnections that are involved.

Building a light switch is a simple system. You just need a conductor, bulb, battery, and switch.

But building a computer has tons of parts. In addition to building the computer, you need ongoing maintenance for life. Aka, the software updates I always forget to do.

Complex systems and building/maintaining go together.

A gardener doesn't ever say: 'Okay, when can I stop taking care of the garden?'

The day he stops taking care of the garden is the same day that the garden begins deteriorating.

The day you stop taking care of your body is the same day that the body begins deteriorating.

Bottom line?
Build a complex system.

'Can I build 30 systems?

That's something we need to discuss in the next
section.

85

Designing the Kingpin

You may be tempted to build tons of systems.
'That would mean that I become smarter, right??'
No. Heck, building too many systems is a way to deteriorate the mindset.

It's better when you have a thread of unity that allows you to build other systems.

A modern-day polymath has supreme concentration.
There are 2 types of concentration:

- Micro concentration is when you focus in bursts.
- Macro concentration is when you focus for long time spans.

Micro concentration is known as productivity.
Macro concentration is known as persistence.

Most can do either micro or macro.
Very few can do both.

When you rush to build too many complex systems, you reduce the ability to concentrate.

'Are you saying that I can't build a business **and** my body? Because a business and body are 2 different complex systems.'

You can build both complex systems…. but there is a catch.

'What's the catch?

The catch is to find a **connection** between the 2.

I'll give you an example on how to build both systems.

For the ArmaniTalks business, it's a *business*. I run a media company that sells books, classes, coaching sessions and much more.

That's the business side of it.

As for the body side, I have a lifting routine.

Not going to lie, there was a period when I was slacking on my body. With ArmaniTalks, I'm always consistent in my posting schedule. Never miss a beat.

But with the body? Eh, I wasn't too consistent!! I messed up a few times. That's when I didn't eat right, get my sleep, or consistently lift.

The result was that it became tougher to record YouTube videos.

'Wait a minute. Your YouTube videos are of you sitting on your ass and talking. What does weightlifting have to do with that?'
A lot.

One of the speaking styles that I promote is impromptu speaking.

With impromptu speaking, you speak without any preparation beforehand. With no preparation, you are required to use *more* mental faculties at a rapid rate.

While using the mental faculties, you need to control the breath in a steady motion. The second you lose control over your breath is the second you start feeling physical pain. Muscle cramps, back spasms, stiff face etc.

A video that would initially be tension free was soon becoming painful.

At that moment, I noticed something. The gym and the business of ArmaniTalks were not separate, they were **connected**.

The second that I was able to create a connection between the 2 was the second that I was able to see how they were a part of the same system.

However, the catch is that we need a leader. **There needs to be 1 system that we build all the other systems around.**
This point is crucial.

Because in the real world, a clean 50/50 split rarely exists. 1 side leads and the other side complements.

Look closely at your body parts:

- One palm is slightly bigger than the other palm.
- One eye is slightly bigger than the other eye.
- One foot is slightly bigger than the other foot.

In the real world, 50/50 is an illusion.

Those who try to optimize for a clean 50/50 split notice bizarre outputs that they were not initially expecting. But those who optimize for 1 leader and optimize the rest of the systems around that get better returns in the long run.

Therefore, ArmaniTalks is still number 1, and the gym complements that. This allows for micro and macro levels of concentration.

Jeff Bezos was once asked:
'Jeff, doesn't it feel like Amazon is doing too much?'

That's when he responded with:
'To outsiders, it looks like Amazon is doing a lot. But internally, ALL our moves revolve around customer obsession.'

Customer obsession is their leader system & they build EVERYTHING around that.

From Amazon's products, services, storehouses etc. Everything is built with 1 north star in mind.

This approach leads to micro and macro concentration.

- Micro concentration is represented by their excellent customer service.

- Macro concentration is represented by their constant innovation with new products & services.

This is a company that used to only sell books!

So, you have a system…and another system…and another system…things are getting messy.

1. Spot all the systems.
2. Create 1 kingpin system.
3. Structure *all* other systems to complement the 1 kingpin system.

This philosophy will have you constantly becoming smarter and smarter. It will become hard to stop you. That's when your emotions are going to get involved.

A polymath does not only use their head.
A polymath uses the head and the heart.

Brain-Heart Connection

As of late, there have been studies with the HeartMath institute that has shed research & insight into the intelligence of the heart.

The researchers and scientists have conducted experiments to see what role the heart plays on the brain.

They have done studies showing how the brain waves are influenced when we center our attention on the heart. Jagged brain waves come in sync and harmony through a gratitude practice.

There is some type of intelligence in the heart that we can unlock when concentration is on our side. With concentration, we unlock intuition, creativity, fearlessness and much more.

What separates a modern-day polymath from other types of 'smart people' is the strategic use of emotions.

When I talk about emotions, I don't mean sitting on your butt and crying about your feelings with others. This is often the first image that comes to mind when 'emotional intelligence' is bought up. I'd much rather call it energy intelligence.

This type of intelligence is the key to becoming braver & showing more humility.

2 fields where pride must be controlled is in journalism and science. Both fields are meant to propose a hypothesis after viewing the observable universe.

But the second the data from the experiment is not congruent with the hypothesis is the second the hypothesis should be dropped!

However, plenty of prideful journalists and scientists are nowadays doing the opposite. They are doubling down on faulty assumptions. They are looking to distort the data to fit their hypothesis.

This is silly.

It shows how pride can destroy a person who is aiming to become a master in any field. The intelligence of the heart is not accessed by someone who is prideful.

Becoming secondary to knowledge is the formula for a genius.

With that perspective, it's easier to let go of a hypothesis and narrative which does not match the results.

To unlock the brain-heart communication, you need to:

1. Improve concentration while building a system and expanding it.
2. Control your pride.

Trying to control your pride without building anything is difficult.

That's like telling someone to just stop a bad habit. Some people can do it. Especially if the bad habit has caused them a lot of traumas beforehand.

But most people need to **replace** a bad habit. By replacing the bad habit, it becomes easier to get rid of the bad habit.

I know a guy who stopped smoking cigarettes by reading comic books!!

Similarly, controlling your pride by itself is difficult. It's much easier to be building something where you are constantly being proven wrong.

When you are being proven wrong, it's not in malicious way. It's when you get a lot of information on a topic and think that you have chosen a side. Then suddenly, another side presents itself.

That's when you are like:
'Hm, I can see a case for the other side as well.'

There was a moment when I was seeing a bunch of businessmen on my Twitter feed. Everything they were talking about was business, business & more business. Market research, follow up sequences, optimizing each sale etc.

At first, when I heard that, I was like:
'Okay, that makes sense.'

Over time, I didn't like their content. I noticed everyone was typing like each other. They were a group of puppets & I didn't want to be like them.

One day, I discovered this one poet who talked about being an artist. He was saying a true artist can go against the herd. This allows them to unleash their peak creativity.

When I heard this, I was shocked. This artist was putting a voice to my experiences.

'Yes! Screw these lifeless business puppets. They don't know what true heart is. That's why all their content sounds the same.'

For the next couple of weeks, I started to build a disdain towards a lot of the businessmen because I **identified** as an artist.

One day, I had a friend whose dog was about to die from a serious illness. He asked me for 1200 dollars for his dog's surgery & said he would pay me back.

This was when I was first starting my business and had just spent 5000$ on initial expenses. I looked at my bank account and realized that I couldn't comfortably give him the money. Technically, I could give the loan, but I would feel scared seeing my bank account that low.

Eventually, I decided to give him the money.

Waiting to get paid back felt like hell. I kept wondering:

'When is this guy going to pay me back?'

I didn't really care about his dying dog as much as I cared about my money.

That's when I realized:

'Wait a minute! I see exactly what these business guys are saying.'

Now their monetization strategies began to make much more sense. I realized the volatility of the mind.

When new information is presented, the mind can SUDDENLY change perspective.

- I understood the perspective of the artist.
- I understood the perspective of the businessman.

And most importantly, I understood the 2 fields can coexist together.

'An artist and a businessman coexisting together?'
Yes, it's called an entrepreneur.

- Entrepreneur = Businessman + Artist

A few weeks earlier, I was pitting business and art against each other. Now, I was learning that the 2 could work together.

1 side leads and the other side complements.

This whole experience made me say:
'Yo dummy, don't be so prideful!'

A prideful guy or girl is quick to want to put labels on themselves and identify with something. Humans are naturally recruiters. They want to keep recruiting others to their line of thinking.

The intelligence in the heart can only activate the inner genius when the ego is replaced with true knowledge.

By being in knowledge acquisition mode, it's easier to tame the pride. When taming the pride, it's easier to make connections from a variety of fields.

Your level of genius will correlate with the level of pride that you have controlled.

Problem Solving 101

Problem solving is required for a polymath to emerge.

You may be looking for problem solving strategies first. But what's more important than the strategy is the **attitude** that you have towards problems.

- Problems are a feature of nature, not a bug.

But often, we treat problems like a bug, not a feature.

When we get a problem, we may be like:
'What the heck, how could this possibly happen?'

Bud, it's because it's a feature of reality! A feature means that it is to be expected. If we realize problems are going to always be present, we can replace a:

- Mopey attitude -> Enthusiastic attitude

Which attitude do you think will make it easier to solve problems?
'Enthusiasm, of course.'
Correct!

Set enthusiasm as the intention. With an intent, it becomes easier to spot when we are off target.

Once our attitude is right, it's off to the strategy:
1. Troubleshoot.
2. Articulate the problem.
3. Create direction.
4. Research, experiment & solve.
5. Problems solved, troubleshoot, or contact relevant teams.

1. Troubleshoot

A lot of times, we will want to immediately start fixing things. That may work for small problems. But for complex problems, troubleshooting is a must.

- This is when you are trying to figure out what is wrong.

Either you are asking questions, or you are prodding the system to see what is going on and what is not going on.

An in-depth troubleshooting session will give you more perspective & familiarity with the issue. Often, a lot of problems are solved at this stage.

2. Articulate the problem

The next thing is to articulate the problem. There are a few reasons you want to articulate the problem:

1. Most of problem solving comes down to communication skills. It's mainly a series of engineers talking and clicking buttons.
2. You gain clarity of the issue.
3. If the problem is complex, articulating the problem allows everyone to be on the same page.
4. It's easier to debrief other teams who are contacted to help solve the problem.

Articulating the problem can only happen when we have troubleshooted and have a general to specific understanding of what's going on.

Example:

1. The internet is not working.
2. The internet was not working since 3 pm.
3. We had a server reboot at 3 pm and I believe that's one of the reasons that the internet is not working.

Steps 1 -> 3 is getting more & more specific.

3. Create direction

Direction is:

1. Where you are.
2. Where you need to go.

Example:

1. The internet is not working.
2. The internet should be working.

The direction can be super simple by the way. You don't need to write a thesis paper on it.

'If it's so simple, why even bother with it?'
Because you have direction!!

It's like getting in a car and knowing where you're going to eat vs driving around aimlessly.

4. Research, experiment & solve

This is the stage where we are going to experiment.

If this is a technical problem, you'll often see that there is already a solution for it on Google. Especially with code. If you are debugging code & keep running into an issue, then research the internet. You'll see an almost identical problem & solution has been presented.

Similar with cooking. Say you get dry beef anytime you are cooking beef stew.

Research to see if others had similar problems. Chances are you'll see that there have been **tons** of people who had the same issue.

By the way, the fix is to leave the meat in the pot until the water disappears. A dash of vinegar helps soften up the meat too! As you can tell, this was a problem I experienced firsthand.

The more creative the problem, the more you need to experiment. A clean-cut response may not always be available on the internet for creative problems.

Let's say you are unable to create the ending of your fiction book. There is no Google article with the ending of your book solved for you. Others can inspire you, sure. But in this case, you need to experiment by writing more.

Maybe create multiple endings & see which one you vibe with the most.

5. Problems Solved, troubleshoot, or contact relevant teams

At this point, for a lot of people, the problem will be solved.

For others, the problem is not solved. You need to go back to the beginning and start troubleshooting some more.

And for others, you don't need to be solving the problem. Instead, you need to contact the relevant teams to get the problem solved. This is why you wanted to have the problem articulated beforehand.

- A dummy gets pissed when they have a problem.
- A smart person gets pissed when they have a problem. Then they realize problems are a feature of reality and there is no running away. That's when they shift their attitude towards enthusiasm & solve the problem to **sharpen** their problem-solving skills.

Learn to spot problems.

Learn solve problems.

Learn to monetize the problems that you solved.

The Scientific Method

Throughout the process of building systems, solving problems, cross combining subjects and more, it'll help if you have some frameworks to codify your experiences into reliable knowledge.

This is where the scientific method comes in.

'Ah…The scientific method?? I want to learn, not play with chemicals in a lab somewhere.'

Learning is what the scientific method is for!

The scientific method is not only for academics and a select few. It's for anyone who wants to systematically satisfy their curiosities and level up.

Here are a few of the basic steps for the scientific method:
1. Observe the world around you.
2. Spot a problem or gap in understanding.
3. Create a hypothesis of the problem.
4. Run experiments & gather data.
5. Assess your results.
6. Communicate your results.

Since this is an ArmaniTalks book, I'm going to give you a direct experience of me using the scientific method. By the way, you'll notice I tell a lot of anecdotes in my books. There is a specific reason why I tell anecdotes. I'm also going to share why you should tell anecdotes too in a later section.

Growing up, I hated eye contact. It would make me very uncomfortable.

At age 16, I was skinny, had no style and was shy as well. So, eye contact felt uncomfortable. Maybe because my self-esteem was low.

By the time I was 26, I built much more confidence, muscle mass and style. Eye contact was no longer an issue.

That's when I noticed when I would talk to people, there were 2 different groups:
   1.   One group enjoyed eye contact with me.
   2.   The other group displayed nervous body language.

Even though at age 26 I was not nervous with eye contact, I had a data point from my 16-year-old self that did hate eye contact.

After observing the world around me, I created a hypothesis:

- Eye contact is not meant to be fixed. Instead, it's meant to be dynamic. Hold strong eye contact with confident people and have frequent eye breaks with socially anxious people.

I never read about this hypothesis in a book. Therefore, I needed to run some experiments.

For the next couple of years, I collected more data, talked to a variety of people, and played around with different eye contact moves.

After 2 years….

'2 years?! You collected data for that long?'

It's not like I stopped my entire life to just run this scientific experiment. Instead, this experiment was integrated into my life with learning and developing as a person.

After 2 years, I analyzed the results. That's when I had 3 options:

1. Get more data.
2. Results suggest that the hypothesis is false.
3. Results suggest that the hypothesis is true.

After analyzing the results, I learned that the hypothesis was true.

- With confident people, hold eye contact as long as you wish.
- With socially anxious people, have frequent eye contact breaks.

This is not only something that worked for me. I *communicated* the results to my ArmaniTalks newsletter, YouTube channel and podcast.

Others tested the results for themselves & got back to me.

They said they noticed a significant building of rapport after taking more eye breaks with their socially anxious coworkers & peers.

'Are the results forever set in stone?'

No. The results from the experiments are not meant to be set in stone. It's meant to be constantly challenged and updated with new information.

This insight of eye contact being dynamic is simply a formula.

A formula is a concept that provides useful value to humans.

This eye contact experiment is a real–world look into the scientific method being applicable to everyday living. The scientific method gives us a simple system to create meaning to our data.

Imagine if you're not building anything. No physique, business, garden, family unit…
Nothing.

That's when you develop a bitter attitude towards problems. The last thing you'd want to do is apply the scientific method.

But when you are building something and using the scientific method to solve real world problems, problem solving becomes fun.

On Google, an anecdote is defined as:
'A short amusing or interesting story about a real incident or person.'

This is when you may be like:
'Wait a minute. Scientific method & anecdotes working together? No way.'

The last step of the scientific method is to communicate the results.

Sure, you can communicate the results with formulas, plots & charts. But being able to creatively connect the content to yourself shows true understanding of the topic.

Not only do you understand the topic, but your neural pathways rewire to *apply* the knowledge.

- Anecdotes and analogies speak to the subconscious mind.
- The subconscious mind is responsible for executing 95% of your behavior.

Since I retold the anecdote of my insight with dynamic eye contact, I didn't have to think twice about implementing the knowledge in the future. It became a no brainer at that point.

When you have used logic and problem solving from the scientific method to gather insights, use anecdotes to communicate the message.

You don't always have to communicate the message to others. You can use the message to communicate to yourself.

I guarantee you do **not** want to sleep on this advice. You will never find this advice in another book.

Scientific method and anecdotes? This Armani guy is crazy!

Not at all. I guarantee you'll have behavioral changes this way.

The 4 components of the mind are:
- Memory – Database of experiences.
- Intellect – Critical thinking faculties.
- Identity – Sense of self.
- Sensory processing system – ability to distinguish objects.

When you go from the beginning of the scientific method to the anecdotes portion, you engage ALL 4 components of the mind!!

When you skip the anecdotes portions, you are missing out on engaging the identity.

The human learns information best when it's personalized. So, personalize the information once you have extracted useful knowledge from the scientific method.

Anecdotes

Information that is personalized is information that is remembered for life. That's where anecdotes come in. Anecdotes:

- Show that you have skin in the game.
- Makes the information sticky.

Emotions play a big role on which information will be sticky and which will not. An example is your name vs a name you've never heard before.

A collection of letters are put together.

But the main difference is the **feelings** that you get from the string of letters that match your name vs the non-recognizable name.

What about 9/11? Do you remember that day? If you're at least a 90s baby, then chances are you recall the *exact* place you were when you heard about 9/11.

I remember because I was in the 5th grade and the teacher was shocked. She wouldn't tell us exactly what happened. But her shocked face spoke volumes.

What about *any* heartbreaking moment? Do you recall that?

Emotions are like a spectrum. The highest emotions are the ones that cause us the most joy (gratitude, love & hope). It allows us to feel good physically, mentally, and spiritually. On the other hand, the bottom of the spectrum are the emotions which cause us to feel 20x smaller (fear, sadness & anxiety).

The modern polymath uses **all** emotions to understand information.

This is where anecdotes come in.

Not only do you bring the information to life from your worldview, but you also make the content **stick**.

To test this theory, get a concept that you know very well. Then tell a story on it with the intention of making me laugh.

Simply by setting the **intention** to make me laugh, you are attaching humor to the information which helps construct a mnemonic. Mnemonics are mental tools which help with recalling information. There are different mnemonics out there.

- Assigning emotions to content to remember something.
- Making something rhyme.
- Using the information in a story to teach.

One reason students struggle in school is because they are being taught information without being explained how the content is relevant to them.

If they knew the relevance, then it would be much easier to remember and implement the material.

How to Create Anecdotes

To create anecdotes, start with yourself first. When you start with yourself, you speak the language of your world view.

Let's say you're an upcoming writer who doesn't know anything about the self-publishing business model.

You heard that Amazon made it easier for independent authors to publish their books. But other than that, you don't know anything else.

Luckily, you had a podcast coach who created a short book on Amazon talking about how to start a podcast.

You look to him to understand how the Amazon game works. Once he tells you, you feel enthusiastic because you realize publishing a book isn't a scary process as you initially thought.

You spend the next few months writing a manuscript, getting a cover made, getting the book formatted and much more.

From there, you publish your first ever book!

As you recall back on the experience, you realize publishing the book was a hell of a process. Not easy as initially imagined.

The first time you wrote your manuscript, you edited some paragraphs out and accidentally saved it. This caused you to have to write many parts over again.

Also, you learned how you were required to be a coach and a businessman while publishing a book. A lot of your consultants need to be negotiated with & coached to make sure they are following instructions accordingly.

And finally, the guy who proofread your book missed so many of the grammar errors! Why were you even paying him for? Should you scold him or be understanding? Decisions decisions…

In the future, when someone asks about your book, you don't sound like a Google document to them.

Instead, you are a personalized database of what it's like to publish a book on Amazon.

Creating a practical anecdote filled with logic shows skin in the game.

Others will benefit from your skin in the game because you can speak of issues in human terms, rather than sounding like a procedure.

Leveraging Neuroscience to Your Favor

I'm certain more people would take learning seriously if they understood that they were rewiring themselves.

Neuroscience is the study of the nervous system. Neurons are the brain cells which communicate through synapses to create neural pathways. The more the set of neural pathways are repeated, the more that you become a new person.

Picture neural pathways like walking in a forest.

At first, when you walk in a forest, the grass barely shows your footprints.

But the more you keep walking the **same path** over and over again, the more your footprints start to show in the forest. After multiple repetitions, there is a clean path ingrained in the forest.

If others were to come to the forest, they could easily spot the path that you created. There are in-depth grooves of footprints on the path.

The forest example is similar to learning.

You aren't just learning the information and leaving it in your mind. That's like knowing the direction to walk in the forest, but never walking the path!

As you keep repeating the information repeatedly, the nervous system begins to alter.

This is a **mind-blowing** concept because neuroplasticity shows that the brain is constantly capable of changing.

Imagine a wizard comes to your house one day and gives you a USB drive. In this USB drive, there is a story about a shy kid who decides to become a public speaker.

At first, when you consume this story, you are hooked.

Your little bother is supposed to be home next week. You want him to read this story too.

But there is a problem.
'What's the problem?'

There are a few grammar mistakes in the story. Also, you believe you could have made the plot a lot better.

Unfortunately, you can't do anything about it…

You just keep going over the same mistakes and dwelling on the additional storylines you could have incorporated.

What now?

Eventually, the wizard comes back and is like:
'How'd you like the story?'

You tell him that it was *okay*, but you could've made it *great* if you wrote the story.

That's when the wizard says:
'Why don't you?'

Why don't you?? you wonder.

The wizard continues:
'Why don't you? You see that **edit** button on top of the document? This will allow you to modify the story as you wish.'

MIND = BLOWN.

- At first, you thought it was a fixed document.
- Now you realize that it's a modifiable document.

That's what it's like when you learn about neuroscience. You learn:

- You aren't a fixed document.
- You are a modifiable document.

You keep creating more content, editing it, and refining the document.

Humans are walking, talking books!

- Our covers are different.
- Our mental contents are different.
- But ultimately, it's the same author.

Viewing humans as books makes it is easier to digest the ambiguous field of neurolinguistics.

What's even more miraculous is that these books are not fixed. They are moldable and are looking for the author (us) to rewrite the story.

How to Execute Deliberate Practice

To learn skills and build habits, deliberate practice beats aimless practice.

A piano teacher once talked about how a pianist teaches the student. The pianist hates it when the student is only showing up and aimlessly moving the fingers.

- Moving the fingers is one thing.
- Moving the fingers with the mind present is a completely different ball game.

Deliberate practice is when the mind and body are present. To tame the mind, we must have a dark **and** light view of it.

Dark view so we are not setting the wrong expectations. If you give the mind room to screw around, then it will. Make no mistake about that.

But we want to view the mind in a light way as well because we cultivate optimism to program it at will.

This balance of dark and light is when we eventually unleash productivity.

'What else does viewing the mind in a dark and light way do?'
It allows us to grasp the proper use of time.

A timer and a stopwatch are your best friends with deliberate practice.
These instruments refine you…

When you are first starting a task, you'll probably have no clue how long it takes for you to execute the task. You'll need to collect data to get a rough estimate. This is where the stopwatch will come in.

Thus far, I've released over 300 plus blogs on armanitalks.com.

Before ever writing a blog, I had tons of bloggers give me advice:
'Ah…blogging is so much work. I do endless research, endless writing, and endless proofreading. It takes me 5 weeks to write a blog!'

When I heard that, I was unmotivated. I don't want it to take that long. But then again, I'm a rebel. Just because it took them *5* weeks doesn't mean it will take me *5* weeks.

After writing the first couple of blogs, I began running a stopwatch. From the keyword research to content creation and editing, it took me roughly *1 hour and 35 minutes.*

After a series of reps, I saw that writing a blog takes me ~1 hour & *35* minutes. A great scientist and engineer understands the role of variability.

Think of **ranges** to factor in human error. So, I give myself a range of +10 and -10 minutes for a blog.

Estimated time to finish a blog:

- 1 hour & *25* minutes - 1 hour & *45* minutes.

I set the timer somewhere within that range. This allows me to stay focused as I create the content.

'What happens when you forget to set a timer or stopwatch?'

What happens is that micro distractions become MUCH MORE PROFOUND.

When the timer or stopwatch is on, I don't even think about looking at my phone or surfing the internet.

But when the timer or the stopwatch is not on, that's when I'm much more open to checking my phone and surfing the internet.

Viewing your mind in a dark & light way allows you to intentionally use the timer and stopwatch.

- The dark part of the mind reminds you without guidance, the mind gets distracted.
- The light part of the mind reminds you that with guidance, hyper focus is achieved.

Sometimes, setting the stopwatch is more than enough.

In my book, Level Up Mentality: A guide to Re-Engineer your Mindset for Confidence (currently available on Amazon) I talk about going on a prior day competition with yourself.

The mind is built for competition.

The error is trying to compete with others. Competing with others was relevant in the agrarian and industrial age where resources were scarce. But in the information & storytelling age, competition with your prior day self is the way to go.

If it normally takes me 1 hour and 30 minutes to write a blog, but out of nowhere, it took me 4 hours one day, I'd want to assess the situation.

Maybe the topic was more complex, and the added time was warranted. Or maybe your boy was checking to see if the new season of Squid Games was out & kept getting distracted!

'What happens when I view the mind in an empowering way?'
Viewing the mind in an empowering way allows you to approach each practice session with joy.

Practice with the mind, so overtime, you begin surprising yourself.

In basketball, there is a concept known as a 'heat check.'
This is when a player makes a difficult shot. Then they make another difficult shot. And another and another…

Eventually, the commentator is like:
'Wow! What's happening??'
The basketball player is like:
'Man, I don't even know what is going on!'

'Getting in the zone' is translation for 'surprising yourself.'

Surprising yourself builds an empowering narrative to keep on practicing.

If you have a jaded view of practice, like a robot without any form creativity, then you are not expecting anything. The mind loves pleasant surprises.

Let me give you another scenario.

Let's say you are a single woman. You're last 4 boyfriends were awful. They were physically and emotionally abusive.

To make it worse, they started off as quality gentlemen. But throughout the relationship, their personalities began to go downhill.

So, you are at that stage where you are even more hesitant of trusting someone. You think:
'What's even the point? This clown is going to let me down sooner or later.'

One day, your guardian angel comes and says:

'Within the next 100 days, you will have 20 dates. 19 will be awful. But 1 will be the best date you've ever had. You will end up marrying this person and spending the rest of your life with him. The only catch is that you don't know which date you will find this person on.'

At this point, there's this **enthusiasm** that has been sparked within you! You are more enthusiastic entering each date with the narrative of:
'I wonder if this is the dream guy?'

Your attitude is much better.

This is an extravagant view of practice. Enter each practice session like something miraculous is going to happen.

This doesn't mean that you have to physically act in a different way. Where you are writing a blog like there is a dragon chasing you.

Instead, you are writing the blog expecting yourself to think of riveting ideas that you were not initially expecting. There is fire in your heart.

Each time you are practicing, each time you are rewiring who you are.

Therefore, have a dark and light view of the mind when it comes to practice.

A dark view to hold yourself accountable.
A light view to become limitless.

Creating a Feedback System

With deliberate practice, there is a concept known as a 'feedback system.' The feedback system shares if you are doing something correctly or incorrectly.

It'd be a damn shame if you were practicing incorrectly and wiring faulty neural pathways.

To master skills and build habits, have some sort of feedback system that **objectifies** you.

We normally view life through the 1st person perspective. That's the perspective we are practicing with. To create a feedback system, we need to view ourselves in a 3rd person perspective.

There are 2 predominant feedback systems:
-Mentor
-Information technology

Some fields are best learned with a mentor. This is when a trained individual works with you to see how you can make improvements.

The trained individual works with their student to let the student know if they are executing the moves correctly or incorrectly.

In other fields, a great feedback system is information technology.
Content keeps us working efficiently.

And you can even combine mentors and information technology.

'Can you give me an example of using a mentor and information technology as a feedback system?'
Sure, Toastmasters.

In Toastmasters, you are given a mentor and speech evaluator. Plus, in some clubs, the speeches are recorded.

A kid named Sammy is going to Toastmasters as a guest. Eventually, he becomes a member and decides to give a formal speech.

After each speech, he will be given an evaluation by the assigned evaluator.

The evaluator will give the critique in the sandwich method.

The sandwich method is:

- What the speaker did right.
- What the speaker could improve.
- Reinforce what the speaker did right.

This gives Sammy perspective.

What did Sammy do right?

His story was phenomenal. He has a gift for content creation and painting imagery in someone else's mind.

What can Sammy improve?

2 things:

1. He only looked at the left side of the audience while his back was facing the right side of the audience. It would be wise if he gave attention to the entire audience.
2. He predominantly used his left arm for hand gestures. It would help if he gradually started using his other arm as well to make the message pop.

His mentor also reinforces that Sammy is a great storyteller. The mentor also notices that Sammy has the tendency to look at one side of the audience & predominantly use one hand.

Great, now Sammy is learning!

After the meeting, he goes to the Toastmasters YouTube channel to view his speech.

That's when Sammy SEES HIMSELF predominantly looking at one side of the audience and using one hand. He also notices that his voice is monotoned.

Sammy is creating a lot of potential for massive improvement. It's because he has a mentor & evaluator. Also, he is watching himself as an object rather than experiencing himself as the subject through the use of video.

Here's one catch:

- Pride and feedback systems do NOT go together.

If the evaluator says that Sammy is looking at one side of the audience too much & Sammy is like:
'No, I'm not. You're wrong! And here's why….'
Then pride is getting involved.

One of the reasons that a polymath fails to learn forever is because pride begins creeping in.

That's why emotional intelligence and thick skin is important for learning and unlearning.

Try this out:

- Record a video or a voiceover of yourself. Then watch or listen back to it.

There will be this CRINGING feeling within.

You will physically feel uncomfortable. You may even say:

'I really sound like that?? No, I can't finish anymore of this talk.'

Feel those physical sensations!
That's your pride being tamed by the desire to know more.

Realize what a magical time this is. We can use information technology to chronicle our progress. When we see where we were compared to where we are, our confidence will BOOST.

Mentors are all around us as well. If you have money like that, then sure, spend it on mentors. Also, with tons of social media platforms, there are subject matter experts who are more than happy to give you some quick feedback.

Tons of people hit me on up on my Twitter DMs and are like:

'Yo, I ended up going to Toastmasters after hearing about it from you. Just gave my first speech. Would you mind giving me some feedback on what you think?'

Obviously, be mindful of the other person's time.

Some form of a feedback system will do wonders for your progress. Overtime, you will see yourself embodying the information & becoming polished in no time.

Failing, Gathering Data and Refining

Without skin in the game, the limitless becomes limited. Too often, we separate fields that are meant to operate together.

I used to know a lot of scientists and engineers who didn't like each other.

The engineer would look at the scientist and be like:
'All you do is research & toggle with formulas. You guys don't build anything!'

While the scientists would look at the engineers and be like:
'You barbarians never sit down and learn from the theory we provide y'all!'

Don't separate being a scientist from being an engineer. Combine the 2. The more data that we have, the better off we become.

Nowadays, artificial intelligence and big data are working together. The more big data that you feed artificial intelligence, the more refined the movements of the artificial intelligence becomes.

A synergy is formed.
Same with humans.

The big data includes all our experiences:

- The good, the bad and the ugly.

The artificial intelligence includes our nervous system.

The more content that we have, the more we feed it back to ourselves. The more we feed it back to ourselves, the more refined our moves become.

'Where does the role of thick skin play in all of this, Armani?'
It plays a big role.

Because if you noticed what I said:
All data is good data.

Let's say a business is starting to gather useful data from their past customers. They have machine learning and artificial intelligence software to process that data.

Do you think it would be wise to only feed the artificial intelligence data of the customers who had a positive experience with the business?

Not quite.

A top tier business owner also wants to know about the customers who had an awful experience with the business. Every negative comment, 1 star review and complaint.

-What sort of product did they buy?
-Which representative served them?
-How long did it take to get the issue resolved?

Were these 'bad customers' or 'potential great customers who were given poor service?'

By focusing on **all** the data, the business can make useful changes to the processes, management and/or team for long term growth.

The modern polymath can do the same. When we look at all our data, we can see how to refine our processes.

The modern-day polymath is gifted because they often get criticized the most, but their thick skin doesn't personalize the attacks or feedback.

Look around you…

There are mainstream narratives that look to make others feel helpless and lost. When a person is fearful, they have a reduced decision tree. The decision tree is the number of choices that a person has at their disposal.

To have an expanded decision tree, you must have:
1. A lot of data.
2. Ability to execute on that data.

If Susie's not knowledgeable of the moves she can make, then she will be unable to make the move. If she has read books on the possible moves she can make, but is too scared to make those moves, then the decision tree remains reduced.

However, if she is aware of the moves she can make, and has the guts to execute, then she will continue to expand her possibilities.

When people are scared and acting like victims, that's when the genius within becomes dormant.

This is how the powerful scare people:
1. Incite fear.
2. Reduce decision tree.
3. Control others.
4. Repeat.

'Why do the powerful try to scare people? Don't they want more people in life to succeed?'
Not really.

The powerful are the top players within a system. Within systems, it's much easier to control fragmented groups.

The smart people have expanded decision trees. Which makes it hard to brainwash & scare them with the latest sensationalist headline.

However, some smart people fall for the trap… sad. These smart people are given a frightening narrative, have their decision tree reduced & begin acting dumb.
Controlled.
Checkmate.

This is exactly why emotional control is needed.
Not being able to control emotions impairs judgment.

There are so many fields that we separate when they could be working together:

- Science & engineering
- Sales & marketing
- Business & arts

And:

- Emotions & intellect

Emotions and intellect are meant to work together. From there, it becomes easier to admit when you were wrong or duped.

Keep learning and refining.
'For how long??'
Forever, champ.

Dwelling

Dwelling is when you allow the mind to drift. Normally, this is a bad act and causes anxiety. But with learning, dwelling is an underrated mental technology that will allow the information to become stickier.

'What's the difference between good dwelling and bad dwelling?'

- Bad dwelling is when you are focusing on regrets, what if scenarios and giving yourself a panic attack.
- Good dwelling is when you allow your mind to become fixed in knowledge.

There is only one goal of good dwelling:

- Find ways to personalize the information to **your** life.

Imagine you have been learning about wealth. You read tons of books on the subject, watched YouTube videos, listened to podcasts & much more.

So what?

Now we need to allow the mind to dwell on the subject from multiple angles. This allows you to strip the subject of wealth to the fundamental level and see how it applies to you.

Wealth is not just about getting more money. It's about giving an abundance of value and getting paid for your work. Also, wealth is about learning how to process life in a different way. This is the mindset where you look out for others first and yourself second. Wealth is about getting your time back and having more control over your story.

The more you dwell on the subject, the more the information becomes assimilated into your reality.

View knowledge as wet cement.

Wet cement is great…
But when you allow your mind to dwell on the subject from multiple angles, that's when the wet cement becomes dry.

Dry cement is what builds towers of understanding.

'How should I properly dwell?'
Let's keep it simple:

1. Assign yourself a subject.
2. Set a timer.
3. Then allow your mind to drift.
4. Whenever you begin drifting far away from the subject, gently bring your focus back to the subject.

If you look closely, this is a form of meditation.

Meditation is often associated with meditating on your breath, which is fine.

When you meditate on your breath, you become more present and focused on the moment. But with good dwelling, we are meditating upon knowledge.

When you meditate upon knowledge, you program new neural pathways in your brain & nervous system to unlock a new mode of thinking. When you think about the knowledge, it's easier to execute the behavior.

'Is dwelling needed?'
Nothing in this book is needed. Different people will consume this book in different ways.

But there are certain frameworks which will build a stronger understanding and unlock your inner genius more efficiently.

With good dwelling, practicing is a must.

Anytime you're bored, practice remembering useful information. Whenever you remember information on your own, you are actively bringing it to the front of your mind.

In the initial stages, it will require willpower to actively recall topics. Later, it will feel like light work.

Autopilot status…

The Art of Teaching

Teaching is a part of learning like learning is a part of learning. Yet, it's easy to treat the 2 acts as separate.

Teaching is important because you are reinforcing what you know AND do not know.

If you can communicate your ideas, then you begin developing superpowers. One of those superpowers is to:

- Give someone clarity at will.

Whenever you teach someone a topic, you update their software.

Knowing the information and being able to pass it off to others is a magical experience.

There are 2 predominant ways to teach:

- Mentor/educate a student.
- Create content.

Mentoring someone is a tricky subject. If you just learned how to give a speech & immediately started mentoring someone, then you may be doing the student a disservice. It's because you barely have skin in the game.

'Then what do I do about that?'
Rather than mentoring them, *articulate your experiences.*

This is where anecdotes are clutch. It's because with anecdotes, you are relaying your logical insights from firsthand experiences without trying to be a know it all.

Also, other newbies will appreciate you for it. Because your experiences are giving them insight on what is important to get started with & what isn't. Articulate what you know with the utmost simplicity.

Another strategy is to create content. This is the era where it's easier than ever to create content.

'How does someone go about creating content?'
Tons of options. Writing blogs, recording YouTube videos and podcasts, tweeting etc.

This my advice…
Twitter is one of the **finest** tools in mankind to learn how to explain things.

'Why did you say Twitter and not another platform?'

For 2 reasons:

1. It's simple.
2. It's public.

When something is simple, it's easier to be consistent with it. With a YouTube video, there are more steps needed for publishing. Dress up, set up the lighting, make sure the mic is working, record, fill in the description box & upload.

With Twitter?
You write & click 'tweet.'

Another benefit of Twitter is that it is a public domain. When something is public, you feel more accountable to show up.

With the ArmaniTalks Twitter account, I've written a bare minimum of a tweet every day for 1000+ days. Eventually, the act of writing becomes a habit.

Another thing is that you begin to **attract** a tribe.

Notice what I said:

*   Attract.

Rather than actively trying to build your following by writing what everyone else is writing about, you are leading with the teaching mindset.

This is a phenomenal way to inspire. Others are learning from your experiences and journey towards becoming a polymath.

There are other benefits too.
'Which is??'
You start to think different thoughts over time.

The average bubba is using their social media to consume negative content & feel like a victim. While you are creating the content that you want to consume.

How powerful.

Did I mention that you are engaging neurolinguistics programming?

The brain and words have a linked connection. Like the heads and tails of a coin.

When I say 'zebra', your brain immediately generates an image of a zebra.

If words are so powerful…

And Twitter is the use of words….

Then what do you think happens when you use Twitter to articulate your knowledge?

Think about that…

The Art of Explaining Things Clearly

In 2005, my parents installed a satellite at our house. The satellite allowed us to have way more channels. Who needs cable anyways??

For the first couple of days, I loved the satellite. Couldn't see anything going wrong with it.

Until…
It started to rain.

Since the satellite was placed outside, when it would rain, the TV signal would get distorted.

Eventually, I'd get an error message on the TV that said to 'try again later.' How the hell am I going to watch Everybody Loves Raymond now???

- Satellite without rain = crystal clear TV programs.
- Satellite with rain = distorted TV programs.

It's the same with explaining things.

When explaining something, imagine that there is a satellite on the other person's head.

- Simple speaking = No rain.
- Complex speaking = Rain.

Now imagine their mind as the TV screen.

If you are explaining with the utmost simplicity, then there will be a crystal-clear sitcom playing in their mind.

If you use a bunch of big words, complex jargon & lifeless formulas, then congrats! You have created an error message in their mind.

Explaining things clearly is an art & science.

To explain things clearly, there are 3 steps needed:
1. Know what you're talking about.
2. Meet people where they are.
3. Strategic engagement.

Step 1 is the most important. You can't explain a topic well if you don't know about it.

'How will I know when I know it well enough?'
You don't fully know until you begin explaining it.

When you have been studying the topic, applying it & practicing, then you should have a solid foundation to begin explaining the topic.

Step 2 is to meet people where they are. This is one of the easiest steps to get wrong. Especially, when you know the topic in-depth.

Dumbing yourself down initially hurts the ego.

Dumbing yourself down means to keep the same content & alter the delivery. Simple language allows for more use of analogies, examples, and relevant formulas.

If you aren't teaching a student, but trying to create content which teaches, then give advice to your younger self. This makes it easier to remember where you once were & the difficulties of being a beginner in that field.

Step 3 is strategic engagement.

Reality check, lectures don't work in the real world. 'Why do you think that is?'

Because lectures only engage someone's intellectual mind. To teach someone, you need to engage all parts of them.

Keep them engaged with:
- Any questions?
- Am I making sense?
- Still with me so far?

The more you practice explaining things, the better you get in the habit of turning:
- Complexity into simplicity.

The more you learn how to explain things clearly, the easier it will be to study.

'What does explaining things have to do with studying?'

When you view explaining as a craft, you'll be able to spot quality content from junk.

It'll be easier to scope through fluff when you have experience creating content.

Call that killing 2 birds with 1 stone.

Asking Questions & Answering Questions

Visualization skills is one of the skillsets that my brand covers (falls under creativity). It's much more effective to create content in the mind rather than always relying on notes. I released a few videos on my YouTube channel on how I visualize.

After I published the videos, I got a question from a follower on Twitter who said that he tried to visualize himself, but it would be blurry. I asked him how he warmed up.

That's when he told me he didn't warm up.

I learned that he was trying to visualize himself in 3D imagery but there were 2 problems with that.

1st problem was that he didn't even know how he fully looked. A lot of people do not know how they look. They can identify themselves on a picture, sure. But when asked to close their eyes and reproduce themselves, that's when they are blurry.

The 2nd problem was that he was going straight into advanced moves.

He couldn't envision a still picture of himself, but he was trying to see himself move.

That's like a skinny guy going to the gym to bench 350 pounds but can't even balance the bar.

He asked me for a strategy, so I gave him a strategy.

I told him to get a BIG picture of himself. The face from the picture should be roughly the size of his real face. You can get an image printed like that in any printing office.

From there, he should stare at the picture for 15 minutes a day. Just allow the mind to get absorbed in the picture.

Over time, he will be able to recall that image at will.

Once he can recall the image from the picture, it fools the subconscious mind into thinking that it's really him!! Overtime, it will become easier to make the still image move.

He wanted to improve his visualization skills very badly because he was in a creative field that required output. So, he executed the visualization strategy for 3 months, 15 minutes a day.

Afterwards, he said it was much easier to visualize himself with ease.

His initial question of asking for a strategy allowed me to engineer a plan that was useful to his life.

Answering questions allow you to:
- Explain a topic.
- Reveal your inner engineer.

As long as you are open to answering questions.

I used to get frustrated when people would ask me questions. I thought:
'Really? I explained it so clearly and you STILL have a question?'
But that's a good thing!

Just like there are good confusions and bad confusions, there are bad questions and good questions.

Bad questions are when someone asks:
'What's visualization?'

Either I did not explain that well or the other guy has no clue how to use Google.

But a question that asks about a specific issue is a phenomenal question because it gets us understanding the subject on an in-depth level.

Have you ever wondered what an inventor was?
'An inventor builds stuff.'
Duh… lol. Give me a better definition.

'Hm... I'm stuck. I just stop at the building stuff part.'
An inventor processes new ways of doing things. To get even more specific, they introduce new processes.

With this intention, our mind opens.

New processes, you say?

If you are a subject matter expert who gives a new way to design a speech, then you have just invented a different process. You are an inventor.

From explaining a new technique, the polymath becomes an artistic engineer. This is what content is meant to be:

- Innovative ways of doing something.
- Not regurgitating the same crap to get extra retweets.

The modern-day polymath is centered in their personality. When the personality is the center of gravity, we have a completely different way of *looking* at things.

Let's say others don't jump in your DMs asking you a question. You know who can ask you questions then?
'Who?'
YOU!!!

When you ask yourself questions like:

- Is there a better way of doing this?

You often get a better way of doing it.

The way the ArmaniTalks brand talks about visualization is not the traditional way it's discussed. Normally when people are talking about visualization, they use it for manifestation. Although I think that's great, my technique for visualization is more for content creation.

If I can see the content already in my mind's eye, then I save a ton of time. It's much more effective to visualize the talk & articulate it rather than to spend a long time writing notes, building the speech & then articulating it.

Why would I walk from Florida to New York when I could just fly?

When I saw a lot of other public speakers taking notes and writing everything down, that's when I asked:

'Is there a better way to do this?'

Once I asked the brain the question, the brain outputted an answer over leveraging visualization.

Therefore, when you are teaching, questions come in clutch.

Solidifying Habits

Definitions allow you to have clarity in your work.

- When you don't have a clear definition, you get sloppy movements.
- When you have a clear definition, you get polished movements.

To build better habits, keep clarifying important definitions.

To give you an example:

- Storytelling.

When you think of storytelling, what do you think of?

'One of those, once upon a time, tales?'

That's what I thought too!

When I was first learning storytelling, I thought it was all about being grand. As if I always needed to tell some sort of fairy tale.

As I begin working on the ArmaniTalks brand, I realized the product was stories. I needed to get *specific* on the definition.

I kid you not, but it took hundreds of practice sessions to finally be able to articulate what a story was.

'What was it?'

A story is a connection of ideas.

When I had that definition in place, I felt like I could fly.

People often focus on the medium more than the act. They say:

'I'm a YouTuber, a podcaster, blogger, etc.'

Imagine trying to do all of them at once. Your head will feel like it's about to explode. I'd know because I used to do that.

Once I got clear on my definition of what a **story** was (a connection of ideas) that's when I realized YouTube, podcast and blogs were just the medium to express the story.

Rather than identifying with all those labels, I identified with 'tell stories.'

- Tell stories in YouTube format.
- Tell stories in podcast format.
- Tell stories in blog format.

I'm officially doing 1 act in many ways rather than doing many acts in many ways.

By getting a clarified definition, I was able to focus on the fundamentals.

Whatever your field is, find the water in the field.

Water has multiple uses. You can use it to:
- Brush your teeth.
- Wash your plates.
- Spin a turbine to generate electricity.

The acts are all different, but water remains the same. The main substance is being used for different purposes.

The average learner is learning all these different fields without a sense of harmony. While the modern-day polymath is learning multiple fields while keeping the harmony.
- Clear definitions lead to a crystal-clear mind.
- A crystal-clear mind leads to refined movements.

End Each Day a Bit Smarter

- Average people focus on improving 10% at a time.
- Great people focus on improving 1% at a time.

Imagine ending each day 1% smarter. Imagine the levels of improvement you'll have in a week.

In a week, maybe not much.

But imagine the levels of improvement you'll have in a year?
Decade?
Decades?

Keep the big picture the big picture. Tons of people struggle with anxiety because they don't understand the bigger picture. When they have no understanding of the bigger picture, that's when they rush more.

To make it worse, they don't understand the effect of exponential progress.

- To a loser, 'exponential progress' is only seen as 2 words lumped together.
- To a winner, 'exponential progress' is seen as a magical force.

To unlock exponential progress, end each day a bit smarter. Every time you are learning new content, your brain's neural pathways are rewiring. The more that your brain is rewiring, the more you are changing yourself on a chemical level. How marvelous!

It starts with the **intention** to end each day smarter.

What is your study practice like?

Do you have one?

If not, you may want to cultivate one, homie.

'What if I'm in a corporate position? I don't have the time to study.'

Yes, you do.

In most corporate jobs, you aren't working a full 7-8 hours a day.

Let's say you don't want to aimlessly surf the internet. Well, then study up on the SharePoint. A SharePoint is the database of procedures that the company follows.

Studying the SharePoint allows you to rise faster in the company. Because if you are a socially aware person who knows everything about the company, you immediately command respect.

That's because we respect people who know a lot of relevant information that we deem important.

Each day, if you are just learning 1% more, you'll develop a mega mind soon.

Most workers on the company floor sees separateness. They don't understand how the different teams are connected. But the more you know, the more you see the invisible connections.

'I'm an entrepreneur, not a corporate employee though. Why should I make 1% progress with studying?'
Fam, you said it yourself!
If you're an entrepreneur, then you of all people NEED to be learning every day.

The modern entrepreneur needs to become a polymath, otherwise, their business will fade away. The world is way too complex to *not* be in lifelong learning mode.

By the way, 1% progress is the bare minimum. Once you have activated 1%, overtime, the momentum will have you learning more than that.

Knowledge compounds.
The more you know, the more you can know. That's when processes from other fields serve your current field.

Playing Dumb

In the world of communication skills, playing dumb is a skill.

'Wait a minute, this book is titled the modern-day polymath and you are talking about playing dumb?' Yes.

Playing dumb means a few things. First, allow me to explain what it does not mean.

It does not mean to act like a dummy in front of others. It also does not mean to let others talk over you because you think low of yourself.

Playing dumb means 2 things:

- You remain a lifelong student.
- You are dumb compared to the bigger picture.

Jeff Bezos from Amazon has a saying called the 'founder's mindset.' He said the founder's mindset is born through a polarity:

1. You need tons of hours spent in the field building experience, experimenting &

developing proficiency over the fundamentals.
2. You need to remain a lifelong beginner.

The reason 2 is crucial is because it's easy to execute 1 and act like a hotshot. Especially considering how many hours you put into the field. But the second that you become prideful is the second you stop lifelong learning.

To be a student, you need to remain a lifelong beginner. Each day is day 1.

Another part of dumbing down is simplifying the delivery.

I know this one kid who obsesses over Bitcoin. He not only knows about the field, but he also wants others to know how much he knows about the field.

He explains the field by using big words, fancy jargon, and complex concepts to make others aware of how well versed he is.

Not only is he looking like a buffoon and plummeting his social intelligence, but he is also going against the foundations of the modern-day polymath.

This guy learns to show off rather than learning with the intention of producing practical insights, inventions & output. Big mistake and it's a damn shame!

Be dumb when you compare yourself to the universe.

'How can I know when I am becoming humbler in context to universe?'

Pull out a Word document and write a journal entry on it. Free flow journaling is when you write whatever is on your mind.

Set a timer for 5 minutes to write a full page. No need to focus on perfection, spelling, grammar, and all that.

Ready?
'Yes.'
Go!

5 minutes passes

Are you done?
'Yes, I'm done.'
What do you see?

'I see a bunch of typos, syntax errors and poor grammar.'

Is there some meaning on the content of the free flow journaling session you just had?
'Yes, there is.'
Great, now I want you to clean up the Word document.

As you are cleaning it up, you'll notice that the symbols (words & punctuation) serve a meaning. These are tiny symbols which you used to take for granted. Without certain letters, the entire sentence becomes fragmented.

There's a **big** difference between:

- My dy is ogign fwoll,

And:

- My day is going well.

As you are going through each of the words & fixing up your spelling, you are cleaning up your mind too!

Not only are you the creator of the journal... you are the intelligent designer who structured each of the words, sentences & paragraphs.

A person who is becoming humble in context to the universe is capable of identifying themselves as simply a letter or a comma in context to the **entire** journal entry.

You may resonate more with a different analogy. Maybe gardening is your thing. For you, it may be a flower in context to a garden.

The analogy doesn't really matter. What matters is knowing yourself to be small and big at the same time.

Behind that paradox is where a genius emerges.

The Art of Reviewing the Fundamentals

The fundamentals are the most important concepts in a field.

No matter who you are, you aren't perfect all the time. Key concepts that you know well eventually fades.

To study effectively and learn better, you need to spend time **recalling** information. There are things called mind maps that you can play around with.

'What are mind maps?
It's when you are understanding what is going on in your mind.

There are software's for this. But I like the good old pencil and paper. It feels more personal to me. The 2 steps of mind mapping are:
1. Create boxes of knowledge.
2. Connect boxes of knowledge.

Let's say for the last couple of months, you have been trying to control your emotions after a breakup.

So, you have been learning about a whole bunch of random fields, diving into rabbit holes & following your curiosity.

You create knowledge boxes labeled:
- Breakups
- Psychology
- Subconscious mind
- Toxic personalities
- Narcissistic personality disorder
- Weightlifting
- Gaslighting
- Nightmares

Etc.

Once you have the boxes of knowledge created, is there any way that you can connect them?

Since your post break up, you have been waking up early with nightmares. Instead of lying-in bed and feeling like a hot mess, you go to the gym early.

What happens when you lift those weights?

Feel good chemicals known as 'endorphins' get released in the brain.

Wow!

The knowledge boxes of 'breakups', 'nightmares', and 'weightlifting' have been connected to produce a unique insight.

The insight occurred because you reviewed your knowledge and did a process called externalization.

'What's externalization?'
Externalization is the process of taking what is in your mind and taking it outside of your mind.

Mind maps are a seamless way to recall the information and surprise yourself.

Imagine if you encounter someone who is going through a breakup. They are like:
'Yo bro, after my girl dumped me, I've been unable to sleep.'

That's when you can effortlessly give useful advice packed with logic because you have been through a similar experience:

'Yo, I had the same thing happen to me after my breakup. You should go to the gym. When you lift weights, you release endorphins and will feel good. Much better than dwelling in bed, you know?'

Nothing is more lethal than a well thought out person with skin in the game.

People without skin in the game would be stuck bragging about how they know that the brain releases endorphins after a workout. But they may not know how to link that knowledge with overcoming a breakup.

This is why the modern-day polymath centers themselves on their personality.

In this era, there is too much information out there.

One person will tell you:
'Subject X is the most important!'

Another person will say:
'That's ridiculous. Subject Q is the most important!'

Who is right and who is wrong?

They are both right & wrong at the same time.
Because they are speaking from their experiences.

- They are right in the subject being the
  most important to them.
- They are wrong when they say that the
  subject is the most important for others.

Your personality is king.

Get to know yourself on a deeper level:

- Introspect.
- Externalize.
- Teach.

The better you know yourself, the better you know
the world.

Unlearning

- Learning is done with the head.
- Unlearning is done with the heart.

It's tough to unlearn because it challenges your identity.

If you control your pride, then you won't be surprised when you find yourself making eye contact with some of your flaws. If you are someone who thinks they know it all, then you'll be rattled by making a mistake.

Sometimes, unlearning will happen instantaneously. Where you were presented new information and suddenly are like:
'You know what? That past knowledge was junk!'

But other times, you are directly presented with information by a respectable source and are like:
'Huh? That can't possibly be true.'

This is a judgment call to make.

Just because the modern-day polymath is making their personality the king does not mean they assume they have experienced everything out there.

Learning the art of unlearning is just as important as the art of learning.

There are a few social media apps I look down on. One of those apps is Tik Tok. Anytime I see someone on Tik Tok, I see them acting like a buffoon.

- They are making a goofy face.
- Doing strange challenges.
- And acting unhinged.

I'd never take an app like that seriously!

Imagine my surprise when people who I respected came to me and were like:

'You need to check out Tik Tok, there are tons of content on it that you can learn from.'

Immediately, I wondered:

'What can I possibly learn from that garbage app?'

That's when they'd say:

'No Armani, it's more than that. There is content that is worth checking out. You should really give Tik Tok a chance.'

My bias towards the app was preventing me from giving it a chance.

That's when the respectable people would send me recommendations. Once they sent me the creators, I was shocked.

Plenty of creators on Tik Tok were talking about Bitcoin, real estate, relationships and much more. That's when I suddenly realized:
'Whoa, Tik Tok has a section where you can learn.'

The people who sent me the creators were people who I considered intelligent. When they were making a case for Tik Tok providing useful value, I had to give it a chance.

On the other hand, there were plenty of people who I didn't consider smart telling me to check out the app. But I never gave it a chance because I did not respect the intelligence of the referrer. Even though they were giving the same feedback about Tik Tok as the respectable group!

My blind spot prevented me from reaching an insight much earlier. This was a time a bias prevented me from learning.
Lesson learned.

'Are biases always bad?'

No, not always bad.

- Sometimes, biases prevent you from gaining much needed knowledge.
- Sometimes, biases prevent you from getting brainwashed.

From the Tik Tok example, my bias prevented me from spotting how dynamic the app was. This was a bias that needed correcting.

But want to know about a bias that did not need correcting?

'What?'

Victim mindset.

In my book, Level Up Mentality, I talk about the importance of viewing the mind as a storehouse of infinite potential. The book also looks down on the victim mind. The mind which is always pointing fingers and avoiding accountability.

I know plenty of people with a victim mindset. They come to me and say:

'Armani, you can't do something because of your skin color or accent.'

I'll hear them out due to respect. But eventually, I'm going to be like:
Bye.

That's because I have a bias against a victim mindset.

Especially when I was building ArmaniTalks, there were 2 setbacks of mine that I could have used as an excuse to succumb to the victim mindset.

I do a lot of emceeing in the Tampa Bay area for events.

The speaking field has a problem called, ageism. Ageism is when someone is discriminated due to their age.

When we normally think of ageism, we may think of an elderly person being discriminated against. But it happens to younger people too.

When someone sees a younger person in a knowledge field like public speaking they often think:
'What can this kid possibly teach me? He has barely gone through puberty!'

Ageism is not the only issue. Another setback of mine is that I have an accent.

A logical person will be like:
'Why would he possibly pursue anything speaking related?'

Due to the bias of my mindset against victimhood, I ignored the setbacks. By ignore, I mean that I realized I couldn't do much about it, so I didn't spend too much time thinking about it.

With the mind primed for the operating system of a victor, I was able to create way more opportunities for my life.

This is when a bias led to a positive output.

When we are learning to unlearn, we must identify what we want to unlearn.

Don't just unlearn something because someone else said:
'You need to unlearn it.'

Do you see a need to unlearn it?

Control your ego for a second. If you give this knowledge a chance, will it impact your life in any way?

All biases are not equal.

- Some biases will stunt your growth.
- Some biases will help you push forward even when you were on the verge of giving up.

Global Conversations

There are different platitudes out there.

- Some, I hate.
- Others, I love.

One that I hate is, 'you need to speak up for those who don't have a voice!'

There are a group of people who are in such negative circumstances that they need someone to speak up for them. But if you have an internet connection, then chances are you are not that person.

- You were given a voice.
- Learn to use it.

You know which quote I love?
'What?'
We travel not to escape life but for life not to escape us.'

Not travel aimlessly. But travel to enjoy yourself and understand how people work.

The better you understand how different people work, the easier it is to learn information.

There was a moment when I was living in the Eastern side of the world. The Eastern side of the world has differences from the West.

One of the differences was that the steering wheel in the car was on the right side.
Why?

I didn't know why at the time, nor was it something that I cared about.

When I came to the US, I saw the steering wheel was on the left side. Once I noticed the **contrast**, I saw how people could ride on a completely different side.

That moment taught me about the importance of *contrast*.

If I spent my whole life thinking that the driver's wheel was on the right side, then there was nothing more to know. All the information possible from this content piece was received.

However, once I saw there was a steering wheel on left side, that's when my paradigm shifted entirely. That's when I started to ask questions like:

- Who is right and who is wrong?
- Why didn't they put the steering wheel on the same side?
- Is it difficult to learn to switch sides at a later age?

With just a small amount of contrast, I opened my mind to questions & possibilities that I was not **aware** of before.

The famous filmmaker, Werner Herzog, talked about his 2 rules for filming:

- Read, read, read.
- Travel to more places by foot.

A few years ago, I went to Hawaii and decided that I was going to walk around predominantly by foot.

What is psychology?
It is a systematic study of the mind.

- During moments of traveling, you don't only learn about your mind.
- You learn about other people's minds as well.

While I was in Hawaii, I learned that different people have different definitions of fun.

As I sat by myself for lunch one day, I heard a family arguing about what they wanted to do for the day.

The father and the daughter wanted to sight see. While the mother and the son wanted to do more active activities like surf, zipline and climb mountains.

There interpretations of fun were different:

- One group wanted to observe Hawaii.
- One group wanted to participate with Hawaii.

I'd be remiss if I don't say why I went to Hawaii.

It's because my old school English professor dreamt of climbing this big mountain in Hawaii. Every time he was about to climb it, he panicked and talked himself out of it.

Well, he was going to be attending a conference in Hawaii and was given 1 extra ticket with all expenses paid. He asked a few of his former students if they wanted a full paid trip to Hawaii.

How was I going to turn that down??

The man was 83 years old. He knew he didn't have too much longer to live. He wanted his final years in to be a blast.

- There were some activities which he did with bravery.
- There were some activities where his inner coward came out. That's when he needed a pep talk.

That 4-day Hawaii trip taught me more about life than 12 years in school. You may think that I'm exaggerating, but I'm not.

Learning opportunities are all around us.

The more you shed the limiting belief that learning only happens in closed boundaries, the faster you learn in formal and informal atmospheres.

Incrementally Rewiring your Reality

There is this saying which states that:
'We shape technology then technology shapes us.'

How true.

A similar quote is:
'First we make our habits, then our habits make us.'

Great habits are built from a theme.
- Without the theme, there are a bunch of disjointed movements.
- With a theme, that's when you are engaging effortless productivity.

The purpose of learning is to add order to chaos.

When you are learning effectively, things make sense. But that's also when boundaries begin to disappear. The boundaries disappearing is why fighters can learn from animals.
Why professional video gamers can learn from fighters.

And why a storyteller can learn how to tell stories from making subs.

To master a habit, it's about:
1. Learning the information.
2. Repeating the information.
3. Applying the information.
4. Doing steps 1-3 forever.

This is why competition mind will destruct you. It's because that mindset blinds you from information that can propel you towards greatness.

During my early public speaking days, I was overly competitive. I thought competition meant that I was doing the right thing.

Toastmasters gives ribbons to the best impromptu speaker, planned speaker and evaluator at the end of each meeting. I aimed to win the ribbons by secretly battling others. Anytime I wouldn't win the ribbons, I'd be pissed.

Soon enough, I was creating a separation from myself and the other speakers.

There were speakers in the club who had unique speaking styles. But for me, all I saw them as was competition.

After some time, there were 4 club meeting where I didn't win anything.

So, I'd intently observe what formula would win ribbons. I noticed a lot of speakers who would cry in their talk would win the audience over.
Should I cry in front of the audience too?

Other times, I noticed funny people would win the ribbons.
Hm…should I be funny?

I was structuring the talk with the sole intention of beating others.

Eventually, one day, I realized it was time for a change. No more competition with others.
Instead, I will compete with myself.

4 weeks went by without me wining anything. This time, I appreciated what everyone else bought to the table.

There was a guy named Bevan who would rarely use words. He was a black man, roughly 6'3 and would smile a lot.

I used to be very jealous of him. Because in my logical mind, I was like:

'This is a public speaking club, yet this guy barely speaks! He uses a few words, pauses a whole bunch, and makes animated gestures. Then the audience eats it up. What gives??'

As I was watching from afar, Bevan was teaching me a lesson.

- Public speaking is not only about communicating with someone's ears.
- It's about communicating with someone's eyes as well.

Bevan was a former actor prior to public speaking. So, he understood stage presence and how to control other people's emotions. He was communicating with people's eyes.

As time went by, I started winning my fair share of ribbons again. But this time, I was not competing with others.

'Who cares? Whether you were competing with others or not, the result of the ribbons was the same.'
But there is a big difference, my friend.

- For 1, my perspective was limited.

- For the other, my perspective was expanded.

When I was competing with others, I was blinded from the different ways of communication that was possible. I would have never learned visual communication if I was too busy competing with Bevan the whole time.

Bevan taught me how the imagery was just as important as the words.

What does this mean for you?

In your industry, you may be finding yourself competing with others a lot.

The habits we build are not only a physical thing, but it's also a mental thing as well.

Habits start off as seeds in the mind and then come out as trees, plants, and a garden in the body. Clarifying the vision leads to better habits.

The modern-day polymath is brought down to 1.
'1?'
Yes, it's one grand vision and everything is built from that.

Without building anything, it'd be impossible to focus on anything. You'd be hopping from 1 thought to the next.

195

It's hard to compete against your prior day self if you have no clue what you are competing on.

Therefore, allow the vison to be the north star.

That vision is all that is needed to spot the signal from the noise.

Lifelong Ambition

- Some people think it's difficult to be ambitious.
- But ambitious people find it difficult not to be ambitious.

The physical body is not the only thing prone to gravity. The mind is prone to gravity as well.

To fight gravity, ambition will allow you to fly.

True ambition is when a human resembles a battery. A battery has a negative and a positive sign.

The negative sign is the grounding of the battery. The positive sign allows the pressure to be generated.

One side without the other leads to 0 voltage. 0 voltage leads to 0 direction for the circuit to flow.

But when the negative and the positive sign are in harmony, that's when electricity flows.

Ambition is like this.

Sometimes, I think polymaths are born from simply wanting to know more. Then I'm reminded that they are human batteries.

Whether they are articulating it or not, they are running away from pain as well.

It's because the senses are programmed to run away from pain and run towards pleasure.
But one of the most dangerous mistakes we can make is to despise pain.

Where we have this bitter attitude when we are in pain.
That's not running away from pain, that's suppressing an emotion.

To suppress an emotion is to declare a war that you will always lose.

An emotion that is suppressed goes to the gym and comes back 10 times stronger. It's wiser to work with emotions.

There is a famous quote by Eric Hoffer:

One nightmare that I often have is that I am so behind in my knowledge that it's too late to catch up.

It's happened many times. My journey towards a polymath began young when I was struggling in school. In the beginning of the year, I was extra motivated. Your boy bought the dividers, binders and took clean notes. I would even sit in front of the class.

However, each time there was a section in the class that I didn't fully grasp. I didn't even know how to phrase the question to ask the teacher. This led me to fall behind…

In a subject like differential equations for example, if you don't learn 1 key formula, then chances are that you will not understand a lot of the other sections.

It's like you are on the verge of building this couch you bought from IKEA. Then suddenly, you see 2 parts missing. The parts are tiny, but it's enough to throw off the entire project.

That's how it felt like in school.

So close…*yet so far.*

Once I got in the real world, I saw people getting their jobs taken by automation.

I come from the engineering field. Throughout my career, I saw veterans in the field getting content. They thought because they worked in the company for a long time, that meant they knew more. Their pride in their tenure would eventually be their downfall.

The younger kids from college were soon coming in and changing up the landscape.

There was a guy named Anish in his 60s who installed printers.

He'd spent 3 hours gossiping with others.
3 hours chilling.
2 hours working.
Installing the printers would take a couple of days.

Soon, there was a new kid hired named Juan.

Juan created a PowerShell script that would automate the printer installation job to a matter of seconds.

Upper management saw this and wondered why they should keep Anish around.

Juan looked around the corners while Anish kept bumping into them.

Just like that, a 61-year-old had to pack up his stuff and leave.
Fired.
It's because he got content.

From the battery, Anish only looked at the positive side and ignored the negative side.

I had to put myself in Anish's shoes. What if I'm in the later parts of my life and am unable to learn like I once used to?

Thus far, we talked about the importance of recalling information that you learned.

There's a bonus:
- Recall the dark moment/s from your life.

The moment when things were falling apart.

Due to your lack of knowledge in something, you royally screwed up. Others may have been counting on you. But your lack of knowledge is what caused the problem to persist.

After a long time, you were able to fill in the gaps of understanding. However, the problem could have been solved sooner. Much sooner.

Guess what?

That knowledge was **always** out there.

However, it was you that was unaware. Does that embarrass you?

Great.

Allow yourself to be embarrassed.

In the emotional world, to turn yourself into a battery, we don't suppress emotions. We actively acknowledge the guilt, shame, and horror.

Then we separate ourselves from the pain by going towards a higher ideal.

- The grander the vision, the grander the internal transformation.

From there, we are constantly level up.

Remain hungry for life.

202

All Emotions are Good Emotions

Emotions = Perception + Energy.

If we don't know how to use all emotions, then we will develop a negative bias towards it. Negative emotions will often allow you to learn content better than positive emotions alone.

I know this because I still know how to solve a Rubik's cube because others told me I couldn't.

Negative emotions allow lessons to become stickier.

What really separates street smarts from book smarts? Think about it.

- With book smarts, emotions are not needed.
- While with street smarts, emotions are a must.

I rather hire someone who has felt the entire spectrum of emotions vs the guy who was shielded from it.

To use the entire spectrum of emotions, you need to get to the stage when you are learning to learn and use your experiences as well.

To learn how to learn, be able to see the harmony between the intellect & emotions.

Emotional intelligence is not about crying a lot. Instead, it's about using the emotions and your logical side together to reach stunning insights.

'What do I exactly need to do?'
Learn to sit with your body more.

One of the most underrated meditations is known as body meditations. This is when you sit down and feel the random charges in your body.

Emotions are energy plus perception. The more you know the energy, aka the physical sensations, the easier it is to control the perception.

Therefore, sit with your emotions.

You have tons of opportunities to do this by the way. Anytime you are in a moment of trauma, anger, sadness, or any other dark emotion, do not immediately go for your phone.

Instead, sit with the emotions and get as detailed as you can with the sensations. Getting detailed with the sensations allows the intelligence and the emotions to work together.

The emotions before were seen as one big blob. Now you understand the emotions on a personal level. It's like reading the summary vs reading the entire book.

When I get angry, I feel more sensations on my right shoulder, left arm & chest area. Plus, the body ends up getting warm.
'Wow, that's really detailed.'
I thought I was being vague to not bore you haha.

'Why is knowing your body important?'
It's because a lot of 'smart people' panic when conflict hits them. Emotional disturbance leads to poor critical thinking skills.

Not being able to solve problems at a moment of crisis is like practicing for a game and getting analysis paralysis when the game begins!

We are judged based off the problems that we spot and solve.

The more we run towards problems, the more we create opportunities to be a businessman.

The businessman who gets rich by ethically solving problems is a special kind of genius. Because they are someone who not only solves problems, but they can communicate their message in a way where others are cognizant of the fix as well. Then they get paid.

Money is not a real thing. It's simply an acknowledgement of:
'Wow! You really helped me out.'

Nowadays as a businessperson, you are required to learn *everything*.

In the early 2000s, there were clean barriers among marketing, sales, product development etc. These days, all the departments are capable of being done by 1 person. Especially in the beginning stages of building an empire.

Bootstrapping is a trait of winners.
'Bootstrap?
Yes, that's when you're using your own resources to lay the foundations.

This doesn't only have to be with business by the way. It can also be a general process for life.

How well are you capable of converting resources?

I know this guy who never went to engineering school. Instead, he spent his early years working in a fast-food restaurant as a dish cleaner. He would work hours to save money for rent and more money to save up for his education. He saved money to attend classes and get a certification to become an electrician.

Eventually, he understood how to work on hardware, software, and integrated systems. This led him to get a job in a fine engineering company and work his way up.

Soon, he knew how to fix more issues than a lot of engineers with formal degrees.

Look at the learning journey of this man.
- He got money from a dish washing job.
- Converted that energy of money into knowledge and experience.
- And converted his knowledge and experience into more money.

This is a guy who is resourceful. He put his own resources up to build his equity.

That's skin in the game.

It's hard to trust someone who doesn't have skin in the game in any field or practical experience building something. That's not the politically correct thing to say.

Because here's the thing:

- Intellectually, they know what to do.
- But experientially, they may not have the best judgment.

It's like me getting advice for how to write a book from someone who never wrote a book.

Yes, they know a lot of the processes. But they do not know the emotional side of the field.

An example is a guy who has never written a book giving advice to an upcoming author. The guy who has never written a book is still well versed in the process of how a book is published. He watched a lot of YouTube videos & read a lot of articles on the field.

This 'coach' tells the upcoming author:
'Look buddy, you need to follow your content creation schedule. I don't want to hear any excuses.'

Normally, the upcoming author is great with deadlines. However, the upcoming author keeps missing deadlines when the book is on the verge of being published.

The guy without any skin in the game will be like:
'Come on buddy, what's going on? How come you're not being disciplined? Just finish the writing process.'

But someone with skin in the game will be like:
'This is not an issue with discipline, it's an issue with self-confidence.'

This guy is delaying publishing the book because he may not feel worthy of publishing his book.
He has created a separation from other authors and himself.

He thought others were capable of being authors because they were someone who was worthy of writing. Now as this upcoming author is on the verge of publishing his book, he thinks:

'*No, there has to be something wrong with my book. Let me do more revisions!*'

Which is code for:
'*I don't feel worthy.*'

Someone with skin in the game will be able to spot the issue from 10 miles away.

Not to say that someone without any skin in the game is not worthy of having opinions. Their opinions are more than fine.

But if you're without skin in the game in anything, then you will not know ALL parts of your emotions. The good, bad & dark sides. The sides to you which you didn't even know existed.

Working with your emotions will guarantee that you look at problems from multiple angles to reach stunning conclusions.

Knowledge is interconnected.
Don't be surprised by how much other problems you can solve by only solving one problem.

Focus

When you think of focus, what do you think of?
'I think of someone who is capable of blocking out distractions and focusing on the important stuff.'

I think that's great. However, that definition requires a lot of willpower overtime. What I like better is to assume that you are already focus, and you are unlearning what it means to not be focus. 'Huh??'

Picture a clean plate. You leave this clean plate in the sink for some time, and it will get dirty.

Overtime, the dirty plate is completely unrecognizable.

Is it smart to say that the plate is naturally dirty? *Of course not!*

At a baseline level, the plate is clean and is temporarily dirty. To make it clean again, we need to scrub the dirt away.

It's the same with focus.

At a baseline level, we are focus. But the mind has become distracted because we allowed it to get dirty with the wrong knowledge.

We can clean up the plate (our mind) by unlearning limiting beliefs, competition mentality & a victim attitude.

There was a great quote by Swami Vivekananda which stated:
'To me the very essence of education is concentration of mind, not the collecting of facts. If I had to do my education over again, and had any voice in the matter, I would not study facts at all. I would develop the power of concentration and detachment, and then with a perfect instrument I could collect facts at will.'

Concentration skills allow you to go beyond the noise.

While others are walking around with dirty plated minds, your mind is getting cleaned with each information you consume, recall & practice.

Here's the thing though:
The digital age is set up for you to be a distracted dummy.

The reason distraction is on the rise is because it's easier to control people that way.

Fighters often kick another fighter on the leg to unbalance them, which makes it easier to land the knockout punch.

Mainstream organizations try to ensure that you are unknowingly fighting with your own mind. When you're distracted (unbalanced) it's easier to plant limiting thoughts in your mind.

Concentration skills create a force field around the mind.

Assume that you are already focus. The more you learn, the more you wipe off the gunk of limiting beliefs, distraction & doubt.

Polish up your plate.

Concentration Challenge

Find an ordinary item in your household. Any item will do.

Eraser.

Bottle.

Pen.

Etc.

Then I want you to set a timer for 4 minutes.

Keep focusing on the object of choice.

When your mind wanders away, gently bring it back to the object of choice.

4 minutes.

Go.

Breakdown of the Concentration Challenge

In the last section, I had you focus on only one object and keep bringing your mind back to it. How did you **feel** doing that challenge?

I don't know you, but I will tell you how most people feel.

They feel like they are one with the object.

It's because they are constantly immersing their mind in only 1 object. This will lead to a level of flow, fearlessness, and creativity.

When the mind is immersed in 1 object, that's when it goes beyond the noise.

What also happens is that you'll feel sensations in your body.

Meditation is not just about sitting in a quiet room by yourself.
Instead, it's about making yourself familiar with ___.

Familiar with anything that you keep repeatedly focusing on.

Another empowering definition of meditation is to turn your mind into matter. Then you influence the matter to make better choices.

As you keep bringing the mind back to the object of choice, I'm sure you noticed that you were feeling a lot of charges in your body. This is you linking your body and mind together.

Isn't it crazy how tons of individuals walk around like their body and mind are disconnected?

Mentally, they want to do one thing, but they do another thing.

Intellectually, I'm sure porn addicts know they shouldn't be watching so much porn. However, their body doesn't care.

Their body is like:
'I'll watch all the porn out there and there is nothing you can do to stop me!'

With concentration skills, we find a way to link the mind and body.

When we link the mind and body, that's when we can connect the mental knowledge with the physical nervous system. Embodying the information is when we act it out.

In the concentration challenge from the last section, I wanted to show you what it was like to link the body and mind.

Our awareness allows us to control the mind and body at will.

We just need to understand the value of concentration skills.

- We don't try to concentrate.
- We are concentration & are removing the junk.

Do you know what the word, education, stems from?

It stems from the phrase, educare (or educere), which means:

To lead out.

Lead out what is already within!

No longer is it about memorizing lifeless formulas which do not mean much. Instead, it's about becoming aware of the greatness that is already within.

Unleashing Genius Potential

The human potential....

It's infinite.

Infinite is cool, isn't it?

That's what we practice for. The more we practice, the more we unlock infinite combinations.

- The regular person sets finite goals.
- The modern-day polymath sets infinite goals.

To become a genius and keep the momentum going, we must have the binary understanding that we are either building OR decaying.

Most people in this world are walking zombies. Unfortunately, there are some habits that have been installed so deeply in their body and minds, that they don't bother to question those habits.

Nothing new.

Similar experiences.

They live out their memories into the future.

Luckily, if you are reading this book, you could tell something was wrong. You've realized that habits are reprogrammable. Time to escape the mental rat race.

In information theory, there is a client-server model.

- The client is a computer that requests information.
- The server is the system which delivers the packets of information.

For a centralized model, there are tons of clients trying to access information from a central server.

Without the server, the clients would be sitting ducks.

Likewise, that's what it's like with the modern-day polymath. At first, the journey starts off with us. But overtime, it becomes a different experience.

We are evolving into the server.

Others contact us for content, strategies, wisdom and much more. We are the server to other clients!

By learning how to solve other people's problems, we help others and ourselves along the way.

In a world filled with clients, become the rare server.

Understand you are first learning for yourself, then a legacy is going to naturally emerge. A legacy and a brand are the same thing.

Brands are not built over night, brands are overtime.

Brick-by-brick…

Pursue Curiosity for Life

The day that curiosity dies is the day that your genius is killed.

To keep unleashing your inner genius, keep finding ways to cultivate curiosity.

Leonardo DaVinci would often get curious about the most random of things. He was once curious about how a bird's beak worked.

The more you get curious about random fields, the easier it becomes to add unique combinations to your field.

Due to Leonardo Da Vinci getting curious about so many random things, he was able to create paintings that would put others in awe.

- The average painter was only learning about the painting field.
- While DaVinci was observing the world and documenting it through his art.

Another example of a polymath is Steve Jobs. There was a period where Steve Jobs moved to the East to discover himself.

He spent time with gurus & learned about meditation, intuition & the fundamentals of life.

One thing he learned from his time in the East was the importance of intuition & simplicity.

Once Steve came back to the West, he wanted to see how he could combine his teachings from the East with the technology of the West.

Around that time, the main players in the computer industry had fragmented products. Software and hardware teams world rarely communicate. So, the product was functionable but it wasn't art. Great engineering with clunky user interface.

Steve Jobs cross combined his artistic nature with his technology nature to unify the software, hardware, and content management system under one house, Apple.

This let him take a whole new approach to his products that others couldn't fathom.

- iPhone.
- iPad.
- iPod.

Steve wasn't just a step ahead of his market, he was leaps beyond them.

Steve once said:

'You can't connect the dots looking forward; you can only connect them looking backwards. So, you have to trust that the dots will somehow connect in your future.'

Therefore, allow your curiosity to guide you, my friend. Expect that everything will connect.

Closing Thoughts on The Modern-Day Polymath

There was a time when reading was a rite reserved for the elite.

In that era, the desire for knowledge was high, while accessibility to it was low.

In our era, things have changed.

The desire for knowledge is low, while accessibility to it is high.

I talked to a few people a while back and asked them when was the last time they read a book.
They looked at me puzzled.
They had to think about it.

After thinking for some time, they said:
'I haven't read a book in over a decade.'

Worst, they associated reading as something you do when you're in school, not in the real world.

The architecture of this book was meant to be different from other books on learning & building habits. It's about focusing on ourselves first:

Know thy self.

With a vision that is continually being refined, that's when the learning process becomes fun.

Once we have the grand narrative that we are working on, and setting infinite goals, we begin to blossom.

For far too long, there was a gap between the legends of the past and the students of today.

This book was designed to close the gap.

You can become great in your field.

Studying is the process of creating networks in the mind. When you see how knowledge is connected, that's when everywhere you look, you'll see objects created with other minds (like yours).

What is an entrepreneur? Have your ever thought about that before?

- An entrepreneur is someone who can create & perceive creations.

At a fundamental level, humans are meant to have an entrepreneurial spirit.

The day you stop building anything of value is the day you start feeling incongruent.

We feel off when we don't eat for the day but how do we feel when we don't study for the day?

The 2 may seem incomparable.
But you should feel stranger for not studying than eating!

The information we learn and repeat is the information we are on the way of becoming. In the process of building, we will learn the theory better than just learning the theory through theory.

Because in the process of building, that's when we engage all types of our emotions, memory, problem solving faculties and spatial intelligence.

The modern-day polymath has a category 5 hurricane of a mind that can consume anything in sight. Nothing comes immediately, it's the long bursts of work that makes the small things worth it.

– ARMANITALKS 🎙️🔥

Afterward

Thanks for making it to the end of this book!

In this era, there is so much content that people are stuck on what to do next.

Too much analysis paralysis and not enough bold bets. My goal with this book was to focus on a few timeless learning principles on how to learn better, study effectively, master skills, build habits and become smarter.

There are tons of players in a field. But there are a few people who are working beyond themselves.

The Information Age should have made humans learning machines. However, due to limiting beliefs peddled by society, the masses have talked themselves out of their unlimited possibilities.

Some people put a self-imposed belief over their head and walk around with it.

How ridiculous.

Knowledge is one. But over time, more people started to discover that knowledge through their own experiences. Over more time, the different fields created compartments and the different compartments created different interpretations & language of how everything works.

The polymath dives through the labels and goes back to the source.

If you enjoyed this book and you want more content from the ArmaniTalks brand, be sure to check out armanitalks.com for my latest blogs, podcasts, videos and more.

Also, I have an email list where I send out a new newsletter every day at 7pm est. The newsletter shares practical strategies, stories & insights on improving your communication skills. Join the tribe here:
www.armanitalks.com/newsletter

Have fun learning and break barriers in your field. You'll soon become the gold standard.

www.ingramcontent.com/pod-product-compliance
Lightning Source LLC
Chambersburg PA
CBHW040750120726
48005CB00012B/1135